IMAGES OF WAR

BERLIN

VICTORY IN EUROPE

RARE PHOTOGRAPHS FROM
WARTIME ARCHIVES

NIK CORNISH

Pen & Sword
MILITARY

First published in Great Britain in 2010 by
PEN & SWORD MILITARY
an imprint of
Pen & Sword Books Ltd,
47 Church Street,
Barnsley,
South Yorkshire.
S70 2AS

Copyright © Nik Cornish, 2010

A CIP record for this book is available from the British Library.

ISBN 978 1 84415 9352

The right of Nik Cornish to be identified as Author of this Work has been asserted by him in accordance with the Copyright, Designs and Patents Act 1988.

All rights reserved. No part of this book may be reproduced or transmitted in any form or by any means, electronic or mechanical including photocopying, recording or by any information storage and retrieval system, without permission from the Publisher in writing.

Typeset by S L Menzies-Earl

Printed and bound by CPI UK

Pen & Sword Books Ltd incorporates the Imprints of
Pen & Sword Aviation, Pen & Sword Maritime, Pen & Sword Military, Wharncliffe Local History, Pen & Sword Select, Pen & Sword Military Classics, Leo Cooper, Remember When, Seaforth Publishing and Frontline Publishing.

For a complete list of Pen & Sword titles please contact
Pen & Sword Books Limited
47 Church Street, Barnsley, South Yorkshire, S70 2AS, England
E-mail: enquiries@pen-and-sword.co.uk
Website: www.pen-and-sword.co.uk

Contents

Dedication

Berlin: Victory in Europe is dedicated to Dorothy (my mum), Angie (patient and supportive and who now knows more than she ever wanted to about the subject) and my children, Alex, Charlotte and James.

Preface

The purpose of this book is simple – to present the reader with a concise account of the operations on the Eastern Front that culminated in the fall of the Third Reich's capital, the city of Berlin.

The text will focus on the drive by the Red Army from the east of Warsaw along the line of the Vistula river to the door of Hitler's bunker. Coverage of events elsewhere on the Eastern Front will be limited to those operations that have a direct bearing on the Berlin offensive and to where it is logical to keep the reader informed. Indeed, the images and captions will provide much of the information regarding other areas of the Eastern Front. The majority of the Soviet images have been sourced from Russian archives and museums and few have been published in the west. The German and Axis images are drawn from my personal collection, which has been built up over many years.

Although much has been written regarding the retribution carried out by Soviet troops during the last five months of the war in Europe this narrative will confine itself to the military aspects of the period. The same criteria apply to the political and military considerations governing whether the Anglo–American or Soviet forces should have the honour of taking Fortress Berlin. Both these topics have been thoroughly covered by more learned authors than myself.

Photograph Sources

Nik Cornish at Stavka
All photographs not listed below

Courtesy of the Central Museum of the Armed Forces, Moscow via Nik Cornish
Photographs on pages 9, 10 (top and bottom), 14 (top), 15, 16 (top), 17 (top), 18 (bottom), 19 (top), 20, 22 (bottom), 25, 26, 27 (bottom), 28 (top), 29 (top), 30 (bottom), 31 (top left), 32, 33, 34 (top, centre), 42, 43 (top), 44, 45 (top), 47, 48 (top and bottom), 51, 52 (top), 57 (top), 59 (bottom), 61 (bottom), 66, 67, 70 (bottom), 71 (bottom), 73 (bottom), 81 (bottom), 82 (bottom), 83 (bottom), 88, 92, 98 (top), 99, 102 (top), 104 (top), 105 (top), 106 (top), 112 (top), 113 (top), 132 (bottom), 133, 134, 135, 138, 140.

From the Fonds of the RGAKFD at Krasnogorsk via Nik Cornish
Photographs on pages 10 (centre), 46 (bottom), 48 (centre), 53, 56, 57 (bottom), 58, 62 (top), 70 (top), 72 (bottom), 76 (top), 84 (bottom), 85 (bottom), 87, 90 (top), 91 (top), 100 (bottom), 101 (bottom), 103, 104 (bottom), 105 (bottom), 106 (bottom), 110 (bottom), 113 (bottom), 114 (bottom), 115, 116, 117, 118 (top), 119, 120 (bottom), 123, 124, 125, 126, 128, 132 (top), 136, 137, 139, 141, 142.

Introduction

Germany's victory on the Eastern Front had been in doubt from the day of Sixth Army's surrender at Stalingrad in early February 1943. Recovery from this disaster was temporary, however, as the failure of the Axis offensive at Kursk in July 1943 placed the initiative firmly in the hands of the USSR.

In January 1944 Hitler's forces on the Eastern Front were divided into three sections. Army Group North was responsible for the line from the Baltic coast in suburban Leningrad south to Vitebsk, where the forces of Army Group Centre took over as far as a point north-west of liberated Kiev. Here was the scene of the severest fighting of spring 1944 as Army Group South fell back, leaving the Crimea isolated and Romania threatened.

Army Group North was driven back from Leningrad into Estonia during early 1944. Axis success between 1941 and 1943 had generated a new wave of recruits from the Baltic States of Estonia and Latvia as well as hundreds of thousands of disaffected individuals from various parts of the Soviet empire. Ukrainians, Cossacks and Russians who preferred the 'delights' of Nazism to the known horrors of Stalinist dictatorship signed up to serve in national formations, attached themselves to regular Axis units or joined Ost (East) battalions. In late 1943 many of the latter were sent to serve in western Europe at the same time as the Italian and Spanish troops were returning home. The support of the Finns, Hungarians and Slovaks was questionable and only the Romanians who formed a large part of Army Group South appeared to be reliable.

Following the Allied invasion of Italy during the summer of 1943 Hitler's attention turned more and more to the west. In November that year he issued Directive 51 stating that the Western Front would have priority in arms, men and equipment as it would be possible 'to lose ground [in the east], even on a large scale, without a fatal blow being struck to the nervous system of Germany.' On 26 March 1944 Soviet forces reached the 1940 border with Romania, threatening Germany's best source of oil at Ploesti. With the coming of the thaw, operations on the Eastern Front ground to a halt in the morass of the *rasputitsa* – the muddy season. Both Axis and Soviet forces now prepared themselves for the summer's operations.

However, before the Red Army could unleash its greatest operation of the war to date – Operation Bagration – the Western Allies invaded France, the long-anticipated Second Front was a reality and brought with it Hitler's nightmare scenario, war on two fronts.

Operation Bagration began on 23 June 1944 and within a month had virtually destroyed Army Group Centre, almost isolated Army Group North on the Baltic coast and pushed the front line forward by 560km. The Soviet advance had almost reached East Prussia and men were massing within sight of Warsaw and the tops of the Carpathian Mountains, beyond which lay Slovakia and Hungary. As the summer drew on, Romania was invaded, changed sides and was abandoned by Army Group South. During the course of the next two months Greece and Bulgaria were evacuated and a pro-Allied coup in Slovakia broke out. The fate of the Slovaks who revolted was similar to that of the Polish partisans in Warsaw; they were crushed after a heroic effort. Hungary, ruled by a pro-German fascist regime since May that year, was Germany's only remaining ally as the Finns had also turned on their erstwhile partners during the summer. With the loss of Romania's oil resources Germany was now reliant on synthetic oil production or the tiny oilfield west of Budapest in Hungary. Hitler regarded the retention of Hungary's oil as vital. During the autumn of 1944 Soviet efforts were concentrated in pushing through the Balkans to link up with Tito's partisan movement in Yugoslavia, the push into eastern Hungary and Slovakia and the retention of the their bridgeheads over the Vistula river, which were subjected to furious attacks.

By the middle of 1944 Germany was reduced to calling for 16-year-old volunteers from the Hitler Youth organisation to fill the ranks of its depleted infantry divisions. Youths such as these were drafted into units, such as Volksgrenadier formations, to bring devotion and enthusiasm to the ranks. The Volksgrenadier divisions were supposed to undertake a defensive role. The trainer is showing the recruits how to operate a Panzerfaust anti-tank weapon.

In late September 1944 conscription was extended to include those up to the age of 60. Dozens of so-called Volkssturm battalions were formed. Lacking uniforms, the men were issued with brassards to give them some semblance of belonging to the army. From the outset the Volkssturm was subject to the authority of the Nazi party. Armament was a matter of what was available locally.

With tank desant men clustered behind its turret a T-34 with a long 85mm gun gathers speed during a Soviet operation in the Balkans. Introduced in 1943, the T-34/85 was the equal of Germany's Panther and perfectly capable of destroying the Tiger I. Tank desant men were expected to jump from the tank and engage enemy infantry or gun positions.

Soviet paratroopers, mounted in Lend-Lease US-built M3 half-tracks, set off on a reconnaissance in force somewhere in Poland. The vast number of lorries and vehicles such as these shown gave the Red Army the ability to operate and maintain supply lines over far greater distances than could their Axis opponents. Soviet paratroopers were by 1944 used exclusively for ground operations.

German prisoners of war (POWs) seen during the summer fighting on the Eastern Front. Many would work rebuilding the shattered infrastructure of the USSR for the next decade.

The Red Army crossed the German border, as re-enacted here, briefly in August 1944 but it was not until mid-October that serious fighting began in East Prussia. The Soviets were rebuffed but news of the atrocities committed there was trumpeted far and wide in an attempt to bolster German determination to fight on.

Chapter One

Into the Reich

Ranged along the Eastern Front, from the East Prussian coast to the borders of Yugoslavia, the Red Army presented a series of fronts (army groups). From north to south these were as follows: First Baltic Front, Third Belorussian Front, Second Belorussian Front, First Belorussian Front, First Ukrainian Front, Fourth Ukrainian Front, Second Ukrainian Front and Third Ukrainian Front. Facing them were Germany's Army Group Centre, Army Group A, Army Group Heinrici, Army Group South and Second Panzer Army. Army Group South included the bulk of the Hungarian Army.

During 1943–4 Stalin, as Supreme Commander, had allowed his Front commanders increased autonomy but, as the borders of the Reich hove into sight, he began to reassert his own authority and that of his General Staff (Stavka) as well as increasing the influence of the political commissars (*politruk*). Stalin was dedicated to assuring the USSR was rewarded for its human and economic losses over the past 42 months. The crucial element in that compound was drawing the Balkan and central European states into his sphere of influence. But overriding those factors was the capture of Berlin and the destruction of Nazi Germany.

Hitler, on the other hand, had increased his direct influence on operations at the front, insisting that no ground be given up, even temporarily, but also withdrawing further and further into a world of fantasy where powerful secret weapons would snatch victory from the jaws of defeat. Focussed as he was on events on the Western Front, Hitler had blinded himself to events in the east.

Planning the breaching of Germany's defences and its ultimate destruction was carefully undertaken. Stalin had learned from his mistakes earlier in the war that it was essential not to overextend the supply lines. Therefore, before any operation began it was vital to rebuild and upgrade the transport infrastructure behind the lines. Consequently, hundreds of thousands of POWs and civilians were put to work repairing the destruction wreaked by the retreating Germans. Nothing was to be left to chance as Stavka was convinced that the Germans would fight with fanatical fury once their homeland was in danger.

During October 1944 Stalin began to plan for the invasion of Germany. The Soviets had the choice of two routes. From the south Second, Third and Fourth

Ukrainian fronts could take Budapest, Vienna and Prague, and advance from Bohemia west of the Oder river to Berlin.

However, this would involve much mountainous terrain and horrifically extended supply lines. Fourth Ukrainian Front's slow progress through Slovakia was demonstrating how difficult such a course of action could be. The alternative, using First, Second and Third Belorussian and First Ukrainian fronts driving westwards across Poland and East Prussia, seemed a more feasible route as the land was flatter and the infrastructure already in place. Furthermore, the troops of the latter fronts were rested, having seen action less recently than those to the south.

Following discussions with Zhukov and Rokossovsky at the end of October Stalin concluded that the main blow would be struck to the north and south of Warsaw. Therefore, it was to this end that First Ukrainian and First Belorussian fronts, commanded by marshals Konev and, from November, Zhukov, respectively, would be built up on an unprecedented scale. First Belorussian Front would then attack towards Poznan and First Ukrainian Front would push towards the Oder river north of Breslau. Simultaneously, Third Belorussian Front, supported by Second Belorussian Front, would drive into East Prussia. Both Konev and Zhukov would have to attack out of the three bridgeheads they held across the Vistula river.

In mid-November Stalin informed the relevant Front commanders that the Polish operation would begin between 15 and 20 January 1945 and that they would, having been given their objectives, plan their strategies. Stalin himself took responsibility for co-ordinating all the fronts involved.

As December began so did the movement of men and munitions into the assembly areas of First Belorussian and First Ukrainian fronts. During the next few weeks both fronts were reinforced to an overwhelming degree. By the eve of the offensive the combined strength of both First Ukrainian and First Belorussian fronts was a massive 2,200,000 troops, 4529 tanks, 2500 assault guns, over 28,000 field guns and mortars, almost 5000 anti-tank guns, 2200 Katyusha rocket launchers and some 5000 aircraft.

Ranged against this, Guderian could muster along Army Group A's 700km front, from north of Warsaw into the Carpathian and Beskid mountains, 400,000 men, 5000 guns and mortars, less than 1200 tanks and assault guns and 515 aircraft. When Hitler said, 'The Eastern Front has never before possessed such a strong reserve as now', on 9 January, he was looking at a map dotted with flags indicating burned-out, under-strength, poorly equipped formations that were divisions and corps in name only. Volksgrenadier formations, formed from combed-out factory workers during the summer of 1944, and foreign units such as Vlasov's Russian Liberation Army, made up much of the paper strength that the Fuhrer alluded to.

The commander of Army Group A, General Harpe, led a force that comprised three groups from north to south, Ninth Army, Fourth Panzer, and Army Group Heinrici, which included First Panzer and First Hungarian armies, and Eighteenth Army.

East Prussia and north-eastern Poland was defended by the remains of the old Army Group Centre under General Reinhardt with almost 600,000 men, 700 armoured vehicles and 500 aircraft. It was believed that the heavily fortified and wooded ground of this region would go some way towards offsetting the weakness in armour.

Hitler, frustrated by the failure of the Ardennes offensive, was convinced there would be no Soviet offensive in Poland and was not prepared to believe the intelligence reports of the Red Army's build-up. Indeed, he was preoccupied with the fate of Fortress Budapest and the tiny oilfield to the west of that city. It was to raise the siege of Budapest that he, without discussing the matter with Guderian, transferred IV SS Panzer Corps to Hungary from its position in reserve north of Warsaw.

Whereas the Soviet plan was to attack, the German plan was simply to survive by defending as furiously as possible. But the weakened front was not allowed the privilege of arranging its own defence. The front line was to be thickly held and the reserves, including armoured formations, were to be no more than 25km behind the front line. This was not defence in depth; it was merely a brittle line and one that the Soviets intended to snap in short order.

On 11 January the Germans intercepted a Soviet radio transmission that ominously declared, 'Everything ready'. Indeed, it was.

An image of Colonel General Heinz Guderian, Chief of Staff of the Army General Staff (OKH), taken in less onerous times for Germany. Guderian was responsible for the Eastern Front from 21 July 1944 until 28 March 1945 when Hitler ordered him to take six weeks' sick leave. A master of armoured warfare, Guderian surrendered to the Americans.

The Soviet infantry along the Vistula river passed a reasonably quiet New Year. As one veteran recalled, time was spent, 'making up for lost sleep, examining the weapons for any possible faults...there was no training of any kind.' Here a group of men enjoys a mid-day meal and relatively clement weather.

A German infantry unit moves into its positions near the front line in a forested area along the banks of the Vistula river south of Warsaw during January 1945. The men are collecting their weapons from a pair of the ubiquitous *panje* wagons that supplemented the Wehrmacht's motorised transport due to their unrivalled ability to negotiate the brutal off-road conditions in the east.

Rokossovsky and Zhukov converse, with Konev in the background. These three marshals of the Soviet Union were veterans of the Tsarist Army and upon enrolment in the Red Army had climbed the promotion ladder. As a Pole Rokossovsky was sidelined during the final advance on Berlin as Stalin exploited the rivalry between Konev and Zhukov. Both Rokossovsky and Zhukov were cavalrymen, whereas Konev was a gunner.

The continual stream of reinforcements and material into the rear areas of both First Ukrainian and First Belorussian fronts turned the snow-covered ground into a morass of mud. The strain that movement in such conditions placed on both men and machines is clear from this image. Around-the-clock work to reinstate the railways did somewhat alleviate such problems.

By 1945 the Red Air Force controlled the skies over the Eastern Front. The withdrawal of Luftwaffe units to protect the cities of Germany from the Anglo–American bomber offensive, and the lack of aviation fuel, gave the Soviets the freedom to fly at will and to provide total air cover to the build-up for the offensive. Here a pair of Il-2M Shturmovik aircraft fly over Poland. Both are armed with eight RS-82 rockets for a ground-attack mission, one of which was capable of knocking out a Tiger I or a Panther.

A StuG III Armoured Fighting Vehicle (AFV), partially dug-in on a reverse slope. The side armour skirts have been removed to prevent the tracks and bogie wheels from jamming up with mud and slush. Armed with a high-velocity dual-purpose 75mm gun, it was, in the hands of an experienced crew, an excellent tank-hunter. However, by January 1945 shortages of armoured vehicles had led to an increasing number of such vehicles being included on the roster of the Panzer divisions.

As well as a shortfall in the armour available to them at the Eastern Front, the Germans had a chronic shortage of infantrymen. Those shown here are manhandling a French 75mm gun converted for an anti-tank role.

Despite the relative quiet of the Eastern Front during early January 1945 scouting and reconnaissance continued apace. Here members of the elite *razvedchiki* (scouts) pose for the camera, re-enacting a mission undertaken in advance of the Magnuszew bridgehead, one of the jump-off points for Zhukov's First Belorussian Front, the other being Pulawy, to the south.

A novel way of providing mobility to a German 20mm anti-aircraft gun is shown here. Warmly dressed in a Russian-style *shuba* sheepskin jacket, the gunner has no shield to protect him, nor any visible means of shifting position. Nevertheless he is well-provided with ammunition.

A Tiger I negotiates muddy terrain during one of the three operations mounted in Hungary to raise the siege of Budapest by IV SS Panzer Corps. The 3rd and 5th SS Panzer divisions (*Totenkopf* and *Wiking* respectively), which made up this formation, were relatively well equipped. Their withdrawal from Army Group A on Christmas Day 1944 weakened that area significantly.

A unit of line cavalry, accompanied by their wagon-mounted machine-guns (*Tachanka*), rides past Second Ukrainian Front commander Marshal R. Y. Malinovsky. Part of V Guards Cavalry Corps, these men were in part responsible for stopping the third and final German effort to relieve Budapest in late January 1945.

An artillery unit, part of General I. E. Petrov's Fourth Ukrainian Front, slogs its way up a wooded mountainside somewhere in the Beskid Mountains in north-western Slovakia. The progress of this front had been painfully slow. Petrov's Thirty-Eighth Army was earmarked to give support to the attack on Cracow by First Ukrainian Front, reducing his front's effectiveness. In the face of determined German opposition the operations in Slovakia declined to a stalemate for several weeks.

It was always necessary for the German forces in Poland to be alert to the possibility of partisans mining the roads and railways on which they depended. This was particularly important during periods of thaw as mines laid in better weather were likely to rise to the surface. Here a mine-detecting team proceeds cautiously along a road west of Cracow.

A 152mm Model 1936 gun at maximum elevation prepares to fire a ranging shot. Such heavy artillery pieces were grouped together in specialist formations known as Breakthrough Artillery Divisions. These units were provided with dedicated transport, supply, observation and defensive assets, and operated solely in support of major offensives. The concept of such divisions dated back to the Tsarist army of the First World War.

Mobile broadcasting vehicles such as this one were widely used by Soviet propaganda companies to undermine the morale of German troops. Often their broadcasts consisted of monotonous, mind-numbing recordings designed to lull the opposition into a state of catatonia. Alternatively, captured letters were read out describing conditions on the German home front and detailing the loss of loved ones.

Armoured trains featured in both the Red Army's and the Wehrmacht's inventories. This German model BP-42 is patrolling the rear area of Army Group Centre in East Prussia during January 1945. The value of such weapons systems was debatable in times of fluid warfare due to their obvious limitations and vulnerability.

Such was Germany's manpower crisis that Hitler Youths, such as the pair pictured here, were pressed into the armed forces. In many cases they proved as brave as the hardened veterans whom they served alongside.

'A present for Hitler!'

Chapter Two

The Vistula-Oder Operation

The First Ukrainian Front's artillery began its initial barrage at 05.00 hrs on 12 January. Bursting out of the extensive bridgehead at Sandomierz, Konev's push towards Breslau began wonderfully well. The German first line collapsed under the weight of a full-scale infantry attack, not the usual reconnaissance in force mounted by the Soviets in such operations.

A second barrage at 10.00 hrs took out Fourth Panzer Army's headquarters, over half of its artillery and a quarter of its men, while others fled in panic. By the end of the day First Ukrainian Front had torn a 19km-deep gash across a 40km-wide stretch of Army Group A's line. Into the breach were sent the T-34s of Fourth Guards Tank Army.

Preparing to face this armoured onslaught were the 16th and 17th Panzer divisions of XXIV Panzer Corps, a strong force of 350 tanks. Hamstrung by orders from Berlin to assemble near the town of Kielce, General Nehring, commander of XXIV Panzer, was caught by the speed of the Soviet armoured assault. Several days of confused fighting near the village of Lissow and Kielce itself reduced XXIV Panzer to a shadow of its former strength and Kielce was lost securing Konev's right flank.

To the south of Fourth Panzer Army's line, XLVIII Panzer Corps, which had not one full Panzer division on its strength, was, by the end of 13 January, in total disarray as the Soviets crossed the Nida river en route to Cracow. To the north of the line XLII Corps had collapsed and would eventually link up with the remains of XLVIII Panzer Corps retreating westwards as a part of what became known as Nehring's 'Roving Cauldron'.

The liberation of Cracow and the rapid success of Konev's offensive took Moscow by surprise as much as it horrified the Germans. Stalin and the Stavka responded by setting new goals for First Ukrainian Front, which were Breslau, on the Oder river, and the Reich's second-most productive industrial area after the Ruhr – Upper Silesia. So important an objective was this that Stalin dubbed it 'gold'. Elsewhere too were the Soviets reassessing the tasks given to the Front commanders in light of their achievements.

Zhukov's First Belorussian Front attacked from the Magnuszew bridgehead with the twin objectives of Lodz and Poznan on 14 January. Three infantry armies followed a short but intense bombardment and breached the German line, allowing the armoured exploitation by Second Guards Tank Army to begin earlier than anticipated. By 18.00 hrs Soviet penetration had reached up to 48km into the German rear.

The breakout from Zhukov's smaller bridgehead at Pulawy began on the following day and achieved similar levels of success. Neither attack had the benefit of air support due to snow and fog. Poorly co-ordinated German counterattacks, although quicker off the mark than those against Konev, failed to create more than limited difficulties for the Soviet tidal wave.

The speed of First Belorussian Front's advance equalled that of Konev and First Ukrainian Front, and denied the Germans any opportunity to construct defensive lines along the rivers that traversed this region. Indeed, the Soviets exploited the frozen waterways as roads whilst their engineers provided bridges capable of taking the weight of heavy armoured vehicles. The close support provided by the mine-clearing and bridging teams was vital to sustain the momentum of the advance, which rushed ahead apace as the German situation descended deeper into chaos almost by the hour. Indeed, it was almost a case of 'every man for himself and devil take the hindmost'.

First Belorussian Front's First Guards Tank Army, followed closely by the infantry of Chuikov's Eighth Guards Army, drove towards Lodz, Poland's second city, which was liberated after token resistance on 19 January. However, Poznan, a vital road and rail network junction point, was an altogether different proposition as it was strongly garrisoned and well fortified. Poznan was bypassed by the Guards' tankers, and its capture was left to Chuikov's infantry, who made their first attack on 26 January.

On the Baltic coast, however, things were moving much more slowly for Chernyakhovsky's Third Belorussian Front, which had opened its attack into East Prussia on 13 January with Konigsberg as its main objective. The terrain, marshy and wooded, favoured the Germans, who were also aided by strong defensive positions originally built before 1914, and extended since that time. Grinding through this region courageously defended by locally raised Volkssturm and regular troops occupied much of January but by the 27th a pocket with Konigsberg at its heart was under siege.

Rokossovsky's Second Belorussian Front had two tasks, the first to support Chernyakhovsky's advance into East Prussia, and the second to protect Zhukov's northern flank. The attack began on 14 January and within five days the German line had been broken to a depth of 65km and the East Prussian border was in sight. However, a further mission was assigned to Rokossovsky's forces. Fifth Guards Tank Army was ordered to push on to the Baltic coast and reach Ebling, at the mouth of the Vistula river. This ambitious plan was designed to cut off Army Group Centre from the rest of Germany. The march to the sea began on 23 January.

Konev's tank dash had been equally successful, squeezing German Eighteenth Army out of the Silesian industrial area, which was occupied for a minimal loss of men and production capacity – this was a bitter blow to German munitions production. The pursuit of German forces to the Oder river resulted in the establishment of bridgeheads at Steinau and Ohlau, north and south of Breslau respectively. But Breslau itself, with its road and rail crossings, remained in German hands.

On 2 February Stavka ordered a halt to allow resupply, rest for the men and machines, the mopping up of German stragglers and the re-establishment of order behind the Soviet lines. Berlin, now within 150km of the Red Army, would have to wait. But as the Soviets rested, recuperated and reorganised, so did the ragged remains of Guderian's forces.

A 76mm Model 1939 divisional gun prepares to fire in support of Konev's main infantry assault on 12 January. The Red Army's artillery was a powerful, flexible tool, well-equipped with robust weapons such as this.

Suitably dressed for the weather, Soviet infantry move forward across unspoilt terrain. The second attack by Konev's infantry followed 150m-wide lanes of ground that were specifically left clear of shellfire to ease the assault troops' rapid passage into the German lines.

The grisly reality of war on the Eastern Front: as the men of First Ukrainian Front penetrated deeper into the German tactical zone of defence they could see clear evidence of their artillery's success, and the failure of the 'Fritzes'' defensive methods.

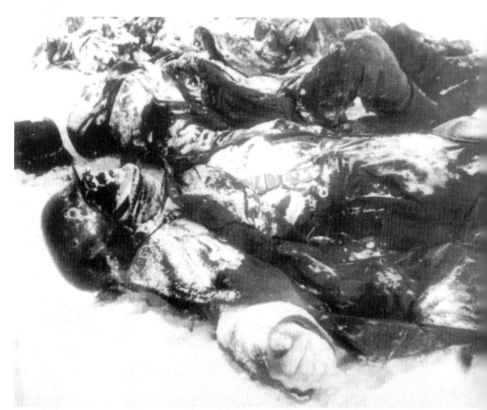

Barely discernable among the trees a trio of German assault guns moves cautiously into firing positions during the Kielce operation. The two Panzer divisions committed over 300 tanks to this action. However, their lack of co-ordination led to severe losses, including one Tiger battalion that was destroyed during refuelling.

A Soviet 82mm Model 1943 battalion mortar prepares to fire in support of an infantry attack. The Soviets made extensive use of such close-support weapons during offensive operations. In wooded areas, firing into the branches of trees to create wooden shrapnel could prove devastating to lightly protected infantry.

T-34/85 tanks and infantry of Zhukov's Second Guards Tank Army go into action on 15 January to exploit the gap torn in the German line. The vehicle on the left has been disabled. On its side is one of the extra fuel tanks often carried. The spongy condition of the ground is obvious from the mud around the road wheels.

Operating an MG-34, German machine-gunners prepare to fire on advancing Soviet infantry. The severity of the weather is apparent judging by the build-up of snow on the men's equipment. Although an excellent weapon, the MG-34 had a tendency to jam in snowy conditions. Groups such as these men guarded the retreat of their comrades by giving covering fire.

The Soviet armoured troops did not have things all their own way. Here a German admires his handiwork with a Panzerfaust anti-tank weapon. His victim is an early production KV-1 heavy tank. The KV-1 remained in service until the end of the war although superseded by more advanced tanks.

Members of the East Prussian Volkssturm take their positions in the line. Fighting on their soil, in defence of their own land, the Volkssturm in East Prussia gave a good account of themselves. Organised in battalion-sized units (roughly 600 men), they often served under retired officers and NCOs who were local men.

During January 1945 the Red Air Force was denied the opportunity to exploit its superiority over the Luftwaffe due to the severity of the weather. Equally problematic was the lack of all-weather runways which made take-off and landing difficult for the less-robust undercarriages of some types of aircraft. The machine shown here is an Il-4 medium bomber.

A Panzer IV with the wider tracks (*Ostketten*), which had been developed to give better performance over snow and soft, muddy ground. The workhorse of the Panzer divisions from 1942 onwards, this version has the long 75mm gun and 5mm armoured skirt around the turret. The unit is unidentified but it is a typical vehicle of the period.

Nearer to the camera two Soviet engineers clear wire obstacles while to the far side a man listens through headphones to his mine detector. Although the German retreat often descended into chaos there were many occasions on which they had the time to mine and booby-trap roads and bunkers. Abandoned equipment was often booby-trapped and Konev's men had orders not to gather souvenirs for fear of booby-traps.

Troopers of the SS Cavalry Division *Maria Theresa* go into action in Budapest. They are wearing the SS camouflage suit that had become widely issued by this stage of the war. The division, formed from Hungarians of German descent (*Volkdeutsche*), was virtually wiped out during the siege of the city.

Warsaw was evacuated by the Germans on 16–17 January with little fighting. The 6th and 2nd Polish divisions, part of First Polish Army, under Zhukov, drove out the German rearguard. Here Polish artillery spotters call in mortar fire to suppress a German machine-gun nest. They are easily recognisable by their distinctive field caps the square-topped *Rogatywka*.

German refugees make their escape from a town in East Prussia. Millions such as these started the journey to the west during the early days of the Soviet offensive. However, there were few if any facilities for their welfare and most of the larger towns' Nazi officials moved them on as soon as possible. This group is passing a cinema and a meeting point for wounded soldiers.

Where tanks and trucks found the going too hard Zhukov and Konev unleashed their cavalry formations. Here a platoon of *Tachanka*, carrying machine-guns and anti-tank rifles, gallop forward to provide covering fire for their sabre-wielding comrades who have passed into the woods to the right. To German civilians all Soviet cavalry were Cossacks and the alarm call '*Der Kossacks kommen!*' sent a chill down the spine of many a refugee, such was their reputation for brutality.

No respite was granted to the retreating Germans. A night-time barrage of Katyusha rockets speeds towards a road junction where a German traffic jam has developed. Organised into Guards Mortar Divisions, they were a less-than-subtle but highly effective weapon with which to saturate an area with explosives very quickly. Lorry-mounted, they rapidly switched locations to avoid retaliatory fire.

A column of Hungarian POWs passes into Soviet captivity. Often guarded by a single Red Army cavalryman, the majority of Hungarian troops were, by this stage of the war, more than willing to surrender if there were no Germans in the vicinity.

Men of Chuikov's Eighth Guards Army deploy during the first attack on Poznan on 26 January. Chuikov's forces included many Stalingrad veterans whose street-fighting experience would be put to good use during the course of the battle to capture the city.

A major problem for the supply branch of the Red Army was the maintenance of river crossings when the weather became milder, as it sometimes did. A pair of Lend-Lease jeeps warily crosses a part-thawed river on the way to the Oder itself. The vast numbers of vehicles provided under the Lend-Lease scheme were almost solely responsible for the speed of the logistical follow-up to both Konev's and Zhukov's offensives.

Panthers and infantry of a *Grossdeutschland* panzer formation prepare to retire to less-open ground near Lodz.

Chapter Three

Stabilisation

In the speech that Hitler made to the German people on 30 January to mark the anniversary of 12 years of Nazi rule, he predicted Germany would be victorious. Within a week the order went out that every German male over the age of 16 would be liable for conscription.

Happily for the Germans, the ice on the Oder river began to melt. The Polish roads, already damaged by the passage of tank-tracks, began to break up and turn to mud, causing delays for the Soviet transport columns.

Guderian, for his part, concluded that the time was ripe for a counterattack into the gap between Zhukov's First Belorussian Front and Rokossovsky's Second Belorussian Front. The original plan, codenamed Operation Solstice, was designed as a two-pronged thrust to cut off the head of First Belorussian Front by means of a pincer movement: one attack by Army Group Vistula, from Pomerania, the other by Army Group Centre, from Glogau, on the Oder river. Reinforcements were to be drawn from Italy, Norway and Courland. Hitler vetoed the large version of this plan but demanded it be reduced to a single thrust by Army Group Vistula leading off from Stargard.

Aggrieved, Guderian set about mustering the forces allocated, none of which came from the fronts he had intended, but which proved to be a motley collection of Waffen SS infantry divisions raised mainly in western Europe from fascist sympathisers. No longer the elite volunteers of earlier days, these formations were divisions in name only and remarkably lucky if they numbered more than 4000 to 5000 men with but a tithe of the equipment due to such a formation. However, the armoured element of the strike force, two Panzer divisions, were somewhere approaching 70 per cent of their strength and they were tasked with attacking from the right flank, with the infantry to their left.

The first attack began on 15 February, spearheaded by the 11th SS Division *Nordland*, probably the strongest of the infantry units. Some success was achieved but Zhukov hit back strongly and the counterattack was called off after three days. However, it did confirm to Zhukov and Stalin that Pomerania and East Prussia needed to be 'tidied up' before any more thought was given to assaulting Berlin.

Konev's First Ukrainian Front began a limited offensive to advance his position up to the Neisse river and take Breslau. However, Stalin warned Konev to keep a watchful eye on his left flank as no clear intelligence had emerged regarding the whereabouts of Sixth SS Panzer Army.

Konev had already been taken by surprise days before by a series of counterattacks mounted by the revived XXIV Panzer and *Grossdeutschland* corps, which had caused havoc in the rear areas of Fourth Guards Tank Army.

The offensive jumped off from the Steinau bridgehead, cutting off the German bridgehead at Breslau within a week and expanding Konev's enclave on the west bank of the Oder river to some 930 square kilometres. Pushing on to the Neisse river, First Ukrainian Front established itself along some 100km of that river's bank and within sight of the Sudeten Mountains. Konev now aligned his front with Zhukov's to present a continuous front line. This Lower Silesian operation came to an end on 24 February.

The end of Operation Solstice was followed rapidly by an offensive to clear part of Pomerania and East Prussia, undertaken by Second Belorussian Front, utilising the fresh and newly arrived Nineteenth Army. Although progress was slow it was inexorable and by 1 March German Second Army was almost cut off from Army Group Vistula. On the same day First Belorussian Front joined in and within 36 hours the German position in Pomerania began to unravel. On 4 March First Guards Tank Army reached the Baltic coastline along a remarkable 80km frontage.

German Second Army fell back to the fortified area around Danzig, which the bulk of its troops reached by 7 March. Fortifying the area was made somewhat easier by the spring thaw and the rising river levels, which slowed the Soviet pursuit. Nevertheless Rokossovsky's forces were concentrated around Danzig by mid-March.

Despite desperate German efforts Second Ukrainian Front ground away at the defence system and by 25 March had split the German area into two. Crowded with troops and many thousands of refugees, it was a bomber pilot's dream. By the end of the month only isolated pockets of resistance remained, protected by flooded ground and the naval guns of the Kriegsmarine, who continually plied back and forth lifting refugees and wounded out and bringing in food and munitions. The last enclave held out until 9 May.

Elsewhere, however, the destination and purpose of the enigmatic Sixth SS Panzer Army had finally become clear during February when its I SS Panzer Corps (1st and 12th SS Panzer divisions, *Leibstandarte* and *Hitlerjugend* respectively) opened the first phase of Operation Spring Awakening, codenamed Operation South Wind. The purpose of Operation South Wind was to prepare the ground for Operation Spring Awakening and it began on 17 February.

Over the course of the next week the Soviet bridgehead over the Danube river at Hron was eliminated, thus putting in jeopardy the planned Soviet drive on Vienna, which would have threatened Axis forces in Italy and Yugoslavia with isolation from Germany.

However, German losses of approaching 50 per cent meant that a halt for replenishment of men and machines was essential. Having received a severe censure from Moscow, the Soviet theatre commanders prepared to meet the main German thrust. Tolbukhin, commanding the Third Ukrainian Front, was ordered by Stalin to fight a defensive action. A veteran of the Kursk fighting, Tolbukhin was well aware of the value of defence in depth and made his preparations accordingly. Minefields were liberally sown, anti-tank gun positions dug and camouflaged, and reserves positioned carefully. Across the line, the Germans made their preparations, II SS Panzer Corps (2nd and 9th SS Panzer divisions, *Das Reich* and *Hohenstaufen* respectively) was brought up to supplement the efforts of I SS Panzer Corps. Two other, weaker, operations were planned to divert Soviet attention from the main event but both fizzled out for no apparent gain.

Operation Spring Awakening began on 6 March in the worst possible weather. Sunshine had reduced the ground to a soggy morass and the anticipated panzer dash was reduced to an undignified, costly battle of attrition. After a four-day struggle the Soviet line began to crack, but even the commitment of two further Panzer divisions could not carry the advance any further. Stalled, the Germans debated what to do next, giving Tolbukhin the opportunity to make his move.

Sixth Guards Tank and Ninth Guards armies were launched into the northern flank of the German salient, which began to retire. Now the entire German strike force was in danger of encirclement and only the heroic actions of the SS Panzer divisions kept open a narrow passage between two lakes to allow the bulk of the of the force to escape capture. As it was, much of the heavy equipment was abandoned due to the mud and a lack of fuel.

By the end of March Army Group South and Sixth SS Panzer Army were reduced to a shambles. They attempted to hold the Soviet advance on the Austrian border but, with 'Fortress' Vienna the clear target, were unable to do so. On 13 April the people of Moscow celebrated the fall of the Austrian capital.

On the Baltic coast Zhukov had driven the remnants of Army Group Vistula across the Oder river. Other than the besieged city of Kolberg, the so-called Pomeranian Balcony was cleared. With Konigsberg also under siege East Prussia posed no threat to the Soviet rear. Now Stalin, Stavka, Zhukov and Konev could call a halt, rest their forces and plan the assault on Berlin.

The final call-up of Germany's manpower took place in February 1945. With the Nazi party exerting more pressure on the civilian population and the threat of summary execution for those apparently shirking their duty, men joined up who would otherwise have been exempt. One such group is shown here.

Men of 2nd SS Panzer Division *Das Reich*, recognisable by the divisional marking on the tank's armour, seen under way for Hungary in February 1945. Re-equipped after the Ardennes counterattack, these officers appear to be sitting on a Panzer III.

Posing here with a group of officers, Reichsfuhrer Heinrich Himmler (centre) inspects the anti-tank company of a Waffen SS formation. Himmler's experience of military life had been confined to a clerical position during the First World War. Himmler spent much of his tenure as commander of Army Group Vistula resting in his train and composing draconian orders to deal with cowards and deserters.

The Red Army also faced a growing manpower shortage. During the advance through Ukraine and Belorussia during 1944 it had solved this by conscripting men from liberated areas. The advance through Poland and into Germany freed hundreds of thousands of Soviet POWs, who were enrolled into understrength infantry units. The physical and mental condition of many of these men left much to be desired, as can be seen from this group.

Men of the 28th Waffen SS Division *Wallonie* leave their transport to move into place for Operation Solstice. Elements of this Belgian unit had seen extensive action on both Eastern and Western fronts. At the end of Solstice the division was virtually destroyed covering the retreat of other units across the Altdamm bridge.

A Panther Model D receives attention for mine damage. The repair crew are apparently adjusting the track tension. The 10th SS Panzer Division was well supplied with Panthers but took heavy losses before being transferred to the reserve of Army Group Centre.

Armour and infantry of First Belorussian Front cross a waterway in Pomerania during the counterattack following Operation Solstice. The transportation of infantry on tanks was a well-established practice stemming from a lack of lorries or personnel carriers earlier in the war.

An ISU-152 heavy assault gun unit drives towards Danzig during early March 1945. It is possible that it is part of the 375th Guards Heavy Self-Propelled Artillery Regiment, Third Guards Tank Army. Nicknamed the 'animal hunter' because of its ability to destroy both Tiger and Panther tanks, the ISU-152 was able to fire high-explosive as well as armour-piercing rounds.

Tank crews of the newly arrived Nineteenth Army parade in front of their T-34/85s to receive a mission briefing. At first the Nineteenth's performance was regarded as lacklustre but the replacement of its commanding officer resulted in a higher level of activity.

A StuG III of the SS Panzer Division *Das Reich* moves up to its start line during Operation Spring Awakening. The passengers are carrying marker poles to delineate safe routes through minefields. Hungarian cavalry followed the German advance to flush out any remaining pockets of resistance. Although the AFV had been marked for the Totenkof Division it was common practice for equipment to be interchanged.

Men of the Third Ukrainian Front stroll through the streets of Budapest on the day of its surrender, 14 February. The industrial area, Pest, had been overrun in mid-January but Buda held out until it was clear that the relief efforts had failed. An attempted breakout was made at 20.00 hrs on 11 February but failed, with considerable loss of life.

A common sight across Poland and eastern Germany was that of abandoned vehicles. The shortage of fuel had become crippling and even undamaged, precious armoured vehicles such as these Tiger Is had to be left behind. Naturally, anything that could be was cannibalised to keep similar vehicles battleworthy.

A Soviet machine-gun team on the streets of Vienna: Goebbels noted in his diary, 'Riots have taken place in the former red suburbs of the city and have assumed such proportions that Schirach (the Nazi governor of Vienna) has […placed] himself under the protection of the troops.' The rioting was limited and the ringleaders rounded up and hanged. But with Sixth SS Panzer Army a spent force the defence was bitter but of short duration.

Somewhere on the Eastern Front, in conditions reminiscent of the First World War, a pair of German infantrymen keep a low-profile watch for Soviet tanks or yet another infantry attack.

Army Group North numbered many thousands of volunteers from Estonia and Latvia among its fighting men. The Estonian shown here is probably a member of the 20th Waffen Grenadier Division. This division was partially evacuated to Germany during March 1945, but the bulk of the Army Group, over 250,000 men, remained behind.

For the men of both First Ukrainian and First Belorussian fronts any and every opportunity to rest and relax was grasped with both hands. They knew the test they faced next would mean an end to the war and for some of them the end of a road they had followed from Stalingrad.

The period of rest and relaxation before the attack on Berlin was occasionally graced with a concert from the Red Army's entertainment section. A song-and-dance troupe are shown here entertaining a group of junior officers from an unidentified unit. Russian folk songs were always popular, as was the song that named the weapon Katyusha.

For the staff of Chuikov's Eighth Guards Army there was little time to relax. Groups of officers, such as these, conducted war games and sand-table exercises to ensure that all eventualities were covered. But as von Moltke said, 'No plan survives the first contact with the enemy.'

Looking rather glummer than usual for an official photograph, men of First Guards Tank Army arrive at a small fishing port on the Baltic coast. The first senior officer to arrive, Colonel M. A. Smirnov, presented his corps, army and front commanders with bottles of seawater to mark the occasion.

StuG III assault guns with infantry aboard move up to their start line for a counterattack in Pomerania.

A T-34/76 passes the burning remains of a Tiger I during Konev's drive to the Neisse river. The weather alternated between snow and frost and sunshine and damp.

Chapter Four

The Noose Tightens

Reviewing the situation in Germany during the latter part of March 1945 must have been of great satisfaction to Stalin, the Stavka and the Front commanders.

Army Group North was surrounded in Courland and the evacuation of troops from there was clearly not a priority. Bottled up, as it was, by several Soviet armies, it could render little assistance.

Army Group South was a spent force in the wake of Operation Spring Awakening, and Austria was open to invasion by Third Ukrainian Front. Although Fourth Ukrainian Front was making only slow progress towards Prague the German forces tied down there could not easily be transferred to the main theatre along the line of the Oder–Neisse rivers.

Second and Third Belorussian fronts had Pomerania and East Prussia in such a vice-like grip that it would be impossible for the German forces there to interfere with the rear of either Zhukov's or Konev's fronts, which were now to prepare for the last and greatest offensive of the war in the east – the capture of Berlin.

The Western Allies' crossing of the Rhine river, and the speed of their advance into Germany, slowed down only, so it seemed, by the enthusiasm of their opponents to capitulate, merely intensified Stalin's desire to be first into Berlin.

Zhukov had visited Moscow early in March to discuss the situation, which was eased by the capture of Kustrin on 30 March allowing an expansion of First Belorussian Front's Oder bridgehead. On 1 April both Konev and Zhukov were interviewed by Stalin, who posed the question, 'Well now, who is going to take Berlin, we or the allies?' Both marshals confirmed that they were ready to do so. At that point both were shown the plan which illustrated the scope of the upcoming offensive. The operation would be undertaken along the whole front from the Baltic coast to Gorlitz, in Silesia, and its objective was deceptively simple – the destruction of the entire German defensive network and the capture of Berlin. Following the initial breakthrough, defending groups would be ignored by the tank armies, which would head for the German capital and other goals, leaving the infantry to mop up and follow on. On the right, Rokossovsky's Second Belorussian Front would cross the Oder river near the sea, separate Third Panzer Army from the rest of Army

Group Vistula and protect Zhukov's right flank. Konev's First Ukrainian Front, to Zhukov's left, would cross the Neisse river and aim to link up with the Americans on the Elbe river. Zhukov and First Belorussian Front would smash through Ninth Army and head by the most direct route to Berlin. However, Stalin had modified the demarcation line between Zhukov's and Konev's fronts so that, if appropriate (that is, if Stalin thought so), First Ukrainian Front could divert to the north-west and advance on Berlin. Stalin ended the conference with the words, 'Whoever breaks in first let him take Berlin.' It was to be a race between Zhukov's and Konev's forces and the start date would be no later than 16 April. Rokossovsky was allowed an extra four days to prepare because his forces had to execute an about-face, turn to the west and arrange themselves along the banks of the lower Oder river.

The next two weeks were filled with work as the Red Army swung into its preparations. Infantry armies were shuffled along the line, tanks were prepared and a mountain of ammunition, particularly for the artillery, was brought forward. The Germans could not fail to see what was going on. However, in the words of one Soviet officer, 'No-one seemed to give a damn what the Germans saw.' The greater the visibility of the build-up, the greater the enemy's demoralisation, appeared to be the logic. For those across the swift-flowing Oder the continual stream of lorry-borne reinforcements and munitions must have made them grateful for the milder weather and the snow-melt swollen river that protected them.

Hitler had declared Berlin a fortress in February but had ordered few or no visible preparations for fear of causing public unrest, always a matter of concern to the Fuhrer, particularly as Berlin's population had always maintained an ambivalent attitude to the Nazi government. Goebbels, in his capacity as Gauleiter of Berlin, was partially responsible for some aspects of its defence. In an ironic twist of fate he consulted General Andrei Vlasov, commander of the anti-communist Russian Liberation Army (ROA) and veteran of the successful defence of Moscow in 1941 for advice. Vlasov was unforthcoming. Goebbels' propaganda ministry described the Berlin Defence district as 'a hedgehog position bristling with defences' which was, as the incoming commander, General Helmut Reymann, discovered, total nonsense. Bureaucratic infighting and interdepartmental rivalry had generated nothing tangible in the way of defences and ensured that what little was in hand was almost buried under forms and the correct procedures at what was clearly the eleventh hour.

On 9 March Reymann signed the 'Basic Order for the Preparations to defend the Capital.' When the apocalyptic rhetoric of defence 'to the last man and the last shot…to the utmost…the battle for Berlin can decide the war' is removed, the practicalities were as follows.

The entire city area of 832 square kilometres was to be encircled by an outer defence perimeter at a distance of 32km from the city centre, running for roughly 240km through lakes, marshes, forests, rivers and canals. Within that was the strongest barrier, based on the S-Bahn (the suburban railway network), which ran along embankments or through cuttings providing ready-made ramparts, anti-tank ditches and trenches, as well as areas of marshalling yards, which provided open fields of fire, or concrete and brick workshops and depots to house anti-tank guns and machine nests. The final position was the Citadel, which encompassed the city centre, government buildings and utilised the Landwehr canal and the Spree river. Here was the core of Hitler's empire and his bunker.

The city was divided into eight pie-like segments labelled A–H (there is no apparent significance in the lettering) under the control of an officer with the powers of a divisional commander. But the crux of the defence system's problems was the chronic lack of manpower. Reymann had virtually no infantry other than a few engineers, roughly 60,000 Volkssturm, some policemen and anti-aircraft gunners plus any wounded he could round up from the city's hospitals. The arms available to the Volkssturm consisted in the main of foreign trophies from earlier campaigns, as the Oder Front was given priority regarding munitions. Berlin's infantry would be drawn into the city when the defences along the Oder broke, and by then it would be too late.

As the Soviets prepared, Guderian was replaced by General Krebs, Himmler by General Heinrici, a highly respected defence tactician, who had proved his worth on the Eastern Front since the failure before Moscow. At this point Hitler issued the so-called 'Nero Order', which called for the scorching of the earth before both the Soviet and Allied invaders. But as all concerned realised, it was simply a matter of waiting for the swollen waters of the Oder–Neisse to reduce before the attack came.

Soviet artillery officers with a captured group of rocket launchers, possibly 30cm calibre, in East Prussia. The projectile nearest to the camera has been removed and the officers are inspecting the electrical trigger wires.

The crew of an Il-2 Shturmovik celebrate returning from the first of the Red Air Force's daylight raids over Berlin. The raid began at 11.00 hrs on 28 March and is remembered by many Berliners as a series of low-level strafing runs below the angle of many of the anti-aircraft guns' depression.

For its part the Luftwaffe was denied the opportunity to strike back on any significant scale due to lack of fuel. The priority target was the Soviet build-up opposite Ninth Army in the Kustrin bridgehead, particularly the bridges themselves. Many aircraft such as the Fw-190s and Stukas shown here were abandoned and their crews and technicians sent to the trenches.

The road sign informs Red Army drivers and soldiers that they are within 165km of Berlin – Hitler's Germany – and that there is a nearby post for caring for the wounded.

An instructor explains the rudiments of using the Panzerfaust anti-tank weapon. This remarkably simple to use and mass-produced weapon was issued in millions to Axis troops during the last year of the war. During the Berlin fighting a division (although its numbers were considerably less than 2,000–3,000), armed with two Panzerfaust each, rode around on bicycles hunting T-34s. It was an excellent weapon and highly respected by Soviet tankers.

All major earthmoving equipment and the men to operate it, along with the fuel, had been assigned to building the defences along the Oder river. The needs of Berlin were a secondary consideration.

In the mountains of Czechoslovakia Army Group Centre battled to protect Prague. Here Soviet air power was not a major concern to the Germans, as evidenced by the lack of camouflage on these personnel carriers and the calm manner in which their passengers are watching the skies.

Red Army engineers struggle in the icy waters of the Oder behind the Kustrin bridgehead to maintain one of the newly built bridges that has just suffered a hit by a German bomb.

A column of Lend-Lease Seeps (amphibious Jeeps) moves up to the Oder river. These vehicles were used to patrol the rivers and waterways behind the lines to protect the supply routes against any saboteurs. The second Seep has a Maxim machine-gun on the bonnet although images show the armament to be US Army .30-calibre weapons.

T-34/85s of First Belorussian Front: Zhukov had 3155 tanks and self-propelled guns at his disposal. Such was the air superiority enjoyed by the Allies that Soviet armour carried painted large white crosses as air recognition markings to prevent friendly fire incidents, such as had happened in Yugoslavia.

Soviet infantry move into suburban Breslau, the largest city other than Konigsberg left in German hands by April 1945. Under siege from 15 February to 6 May, Breslau justified Hitler's faith in the concept of fortresses.

A Tiger I moves out cautiously from its tree cover. Army Group Vistula's two component armies, Ninth and Third Panzer, had 754 tanks between them. Four Panzer divisions were transferred to Army Group Vistula, where Hitler's intuition told him the main Soviet thrust would be.

Jubilant men of Third Belorussian Front celebrate the fall of Konigsberg on 9 April. Hitler condemned the garrison commander, General Lasch, to death in his absence. Erich Koch, the Gauleiter of East Prussia, had himself evacuated weeks before. Lasch told his interrogators, 'The fall of Konigsberg will expedite the final collapse'.

Men of Vlasov's Russian Liberation Army, dressed in a mix of Soviet and German uniform, prepare to go into the line. Vlasov's Guard Battalion of Russians carried out a mission on the Oder Front which generated a surprisingly large number of Soviet deserters at this late stage in the war.

The expression on this SS man's face encapsulates the despair felt by many members of the German armed forces during April 1945. No promise of V-weapons or any other last-minute miracle, such as the death of US President Roosevelt on 12 April, was going to prevent the defeat of the Third Reich.

Manoeuvring a ZIS-3 76mm divisional field gun into position under cover was not always an easy task for the crew of five. The gun appears to have slipped off the track into a ditch. Second Belorussian Front was equipped with 6642 guns and mortars, a ninefold superiority over Third Panzer Army.

In position but, as yet, lacking camouflage, is a Soviet ML-20 152mm howitzer of First Ukrainian Front. With a range of some 20km, this piece was capable of hitting anywhere within the Fourth Panzer Army's defensive zone. Part of Army Group Centre, Fourth Panzer Army stood in the path of Konev's drive to the Elbe, Berlin and Dresden.

A young paratrooper, possibly of 9th Parachute Division, part of LVI Panzer Corps, on the Seelow Heights position, looks nervously up at the sky. The Seelow Heights was a crucial part of Ninth Army's defences along the Oder, overlooking the Kustrin bridgehead. Busse, commanding Ninth Army, had some 220,000 men facing three times that number under Zhukov's command.

Chapter Five

Across the Oder-Neisse Line

Hitler's prediction that the attack on Berlin via the Seelow Heights was merely a diversion from the main thrust on Prague was proved false at 03.00 hrs on 16 April when the artillery of First Belorussian Front began its bombardment of the German defences. Zhukov's main attack was aimed at the solidly fortified Seelow Heights, which dominated the Soviet bridgehead in the Oder Valley (Oderbruch) and formed the lynchpin of the Oder line east of Berlin.

The bombardment lasted for 30 minutes, and the moment it ended, the infantrymen of Chuikov's Eighth Guards Army went into action. To support this assault 143 searchlights were turned on to illuminate the German lines and blind the few remaining defenders left in the first line. In fact the lights only silhouetted the attackers and confused their vision as the light reflected haphazardly from the all-consuming dust and smoke. As Eighth Guards stormed forward over the churned and crater-scarred ground, to their left, Thirty-Third and Sixty-Ninth armies moved out to isolate Frankfurt. To the north First and Sixty-First armies crossed the Oder river by all means available, boats, rafts, pontoons and Lend-Lease amphibians, in an attempt to establish bridgeheads.

At first the Eighth Guards' attack made good progress across the marshy ground and up the slopes towards the German first line of fortifications. However, they began to lose impetus due to 'the brooks and canals…deciding to wait for the dawn in order to examine the obstacles they would have to cross', as Chuikov noted in his memoirs. Such delays gave the Germans time to regain their equilibrium, and very quickly their artillery and machine-guns began to pour fire into the Soviets below them. To one German artillery observer the Soviet attack looked like 'one big traffic jam, a marvellous target'. Frustrated, Zhukov ordered another barrage at midday, followed by an attack by the T-34s of First Guards Tank Army, which was not scheduled to advance until the infantry had cleared the way. This operation also became bogged down and the tank losses began to mount. Progress had been marginal all across Zhukov's front. As the day drew to a close Krebs spoke with Heinrici, commander of Army Group Vistula, saying, 'We have good reason to be satisfied.' Heinrici was not so sure. Zhukov, for his part, spoke to Stalin, who hinted that Konev was the favoured candidate for the role of captor of Berlin.

Konev's First Ukrainian Front had achieved considerable success on 16 April. With no bridgeheads over the Neisse river the whole operation was amphibious. Covered by an immense smokescreen almost 400km long and a powerful barrage, men of Thirteenth Army had crossed the Neisse river on anything that would float; indeed, a considerable number of them swam. At 08.45 hrs, two and a half hours into the offensive, 130 crossings had been made along 80km of the front and the engineers were building 30- and 60-ton bridges to carry the armour and artillery forward. By the evening of the first day Konev's bridgehead was already 14km deep and 27km wide, and several counterattacks had been successfully held off. Furthermore, I Guards Cavalry Corps was heading into the Germans' rear areas. Second Polish Army was also under way and making for Dresden. Konev's thrusting performance was rewarded by Stalin, who ordered him, 'Turn your tank armies on Berlin.'

Zhukov's position was not improving. Despite fighting through the night his troops made little headway. The commander of First Guards Tank Army commented that he had not 'seen such resistance in the whole of the war'.

At 10.00 hrs on 17 April Zhukov's artillery again pounded the German lines, while Eighth Guards attacked repeatedly with armoured support. As the German line started to buckle and its gunners began to run out of ammunition reinforcements arrived to stabilise the situation: the 11th SS Panzergrenadier Division *Nordland* and 23rd SS Panzergrenadier Division *Nederland* from Third Panzer Army. It was too little too late. After another day of heavy fighting and lacking ammunition and sufficient reserves Ninth Army's third line of defence disintegrated on 19 April and a 72km gap directly east of Berlin was suddenly open. LVI Corps fell back towards Berlin and XI SS Panzer Corps retired to the south-west.

Meanwhile, First Ukrainian Front's Third and Fourth Guards Tank armies, leaving the infantry formations behind to mop up any serious opposition, drove furiously for south Berlin reaching the capital's ring road on 20 April. Zossen, the nerve centre of the German high command, was occupied by Third Guards Tank Army the following day. However, in the Spree forests near the town of Cottbus, units of Ninth and Fourth Panzer armies were gathering in strength and defending themselves against elements of both First Belorussian and First Ukrainian fronts.

To the north of Zhukov's command Second Belorussian Front, under Rokossovsky, opened its contribution to the Berlin offensive on 20 April, having just completed its monumental regrouping along the banks of the Oder river where the shoreline dissolved into wetlands, marsh and finally the Baltic Sea. It was difficult ground on which to fight. Utilising a 47km-wide smokescreen, Second Belorussian Front's armies began their crossing. Exploiting the achievement of Sixty-Fifth Army, a bridgehead of some 65 square kilometres was developed by 21 April. In the face of this and events to the south, Third Panzer Army retired steadily, shepherding thousands of refugees with them. Rokossovsky told off several units to occupy the islands and cover the coastline to prevent any last-minute landings by the forces of Army Group North.

With the collapse of the Seelow defence system Zhukov had issued orders that Eighth Guards and First Guards Tank armies pursue the Germans along Reichstrasse 1, and cross the Spree and Dahme rivers to strike at Berlin from the south. To the north Second Guards Tank Army would lead Forty-Seventh, Fifth Shock and Third Shock armies into Berlin from the north and north-east. The retreating Germans fought many brutal rearguard actions against all comers gaining valuable time for the forces in Berlin to put their defences in order.

Between 20 and 21 April the British and American air raids on Berlin ceased but 21 April was also marked by events in Hitler's bunker. Possibly prompted by the first Soviet shelling of his capital, Hitler ordered a counterattack to be conducted by Obergruppenfuhrer Felix Steiner's III SS Corps with the aim of smashing Zhukov's right flank as it moved west to link up with Konev's forces. This was rooted in fantasy, as Steiner lacked the wherewithal to do little apart from defend himself. To compound matters Hitler also sacked Reymann, the commander of Berlin. This SS counterattack became the focus of all Hitler's attention for the next 36 hours until he was informed by his senior military advisors that Steiner had not moved. Reportedly Hitler broke down and stated that the war was lost and that he would stay in Berlin, where he would commit suicide rather than face captivity. Eventually he was calmed down by the suggestion that Twelfth Army, holding the Elbe river against the Americans, would regroup and rescue Berlin.

On 22 April Third Guards Tank Army reached the Teltow canal, to the south of Berlin's outer defence perimeter; on its left flank Fourth Guards Tank Army was approaching Potsdam with only 40km separating its left flank from Zhukov's extreme right wing.

The following day, Monday 23 April, Stalin announced the final order for the taking of Berlin. The demarcation line between First Ukrainian and First Belorussian fronts was drawn some 140m west of the Reichstag, which placed it within Zhukov's area of responsibility. Therefore, to Zhukov and his men would go the glory of the final battle, though not all its hardship.

Marshal Georgi Konstantinovitch Zhukov (seated) was an increasingly worried man as his First Belorussian Front's main attack on the Seelow Heights became bogged down during its first day. Zhukov had promised Stalin that the Seelow Heights would be in his hands on 16 April and had not achieved this goal.

First Belorussian Front's artillery opens fire on German positions on the Seelow Heights. However, German troops had been withdrawn from the front-line positions following General Heinrici's orders. Consequently, their losses were not as heavy as those sustained during the bombardment of the Vistula river line three months earlier. Zhukov's gunners used over 1,250,000 rounds on the first day alone.

One of Konev's units marks the point of its newly established bridgeheads on the western bank of the Neisse river. Red flags had been issued for this purpose. The remains of the extensive smoke employed in this operation can be seen behind this man.

Soviet combat engineers struggle with a barbed-wire obstacle in the Oder Valley. To their cost the Soviet senior officers were relearning the lesson of the First World War that heavy artillery bombardments severely damaged the ground over which the attackers were to pass – and did not always smash wire entanglements. The men are wearing camouflage suits reserved for specialists.

In the defensive lines overlooking the Oder river a German officer observes Soviet movements. Both sides carried out combat and reconnaissance patrols during the days that led up to the Soviet offensive. Army Group Vistula received details of Soviet plans the day before it began from a POW.

Reserves being rushed up to the Seelow Heights position on 17 April. Incredibly, the heavily camouflaged lorry to the front has just picked up a camera team from an SS Propaganda unit (note the cameraman standing by the cab door). It was on men such as these that Goebbels' Propaganda Ministry depended for its action footage.

An officer of the *Grossdeutschland* Panzer Corps takes shelter from Soviet artillery fire. Men and vehicles of this elite Wehrmacht unit appeared at various points along the front line although the bulk were now with Army Group Centre facing Konev's advance. An officer of this unit described the Seelow fighting as, 'not a killing field but a slaughterhouse'.

A StuG III moves up through Seelow town to join in with one of the many armoured counterattacks that took place. Groups of German armoured vehicles carried out ambushes that accounted for scores of Soviet tanks during the confusion of the fighting. Particularly active in this role was the 111th Training Brigade.

To the north of Seelow men of Soviet Sixty-First Army embark to cross the Oder in pontoons manned by engineers. The amphibious assault took heavy casualties from concentrated German fire. Of one battalion in the first wave only eight men reached the west bank.

A T-34/85 emerges from the west bank of the Spree river on 17 April. Konev's Fourth Guards Tank Army crossed the Spree at a point where it was a metre deep. The speed of their advance denied Fourth Panzer Army the opportunity to form a cohesive defence line. Army Group Centre was beginning to fall apart.

Paratroopers of the 9th Parachute Division prepare to counterattack on 18 April. They are mounted on a Marder II self-propelled anti-tank gun. The paratroopers of 9th Parachute Division were an elite force in name only, being mainly composed of recently 'combed-out' Luftwaffe ground crew. Their performance during the Seelow fighting was less than glorious; the division broke and ran.

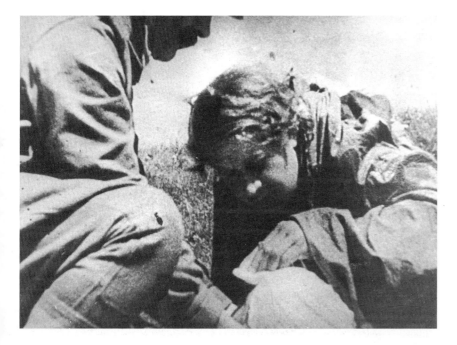

Soviet casualties during the Seelow and Neisse river fighting were high. Casualty evacuation and the treatment of the wounded were areas that the battle's post-war Soviet analysts criticised. Female medical workers in the firing line, such as the one shown here, had been a feature of the Russian military from at least the First World War.

First Ukrainian Front's advance on Dresden was rudely interrupted by what was the last German armoured attack in any strength. Striking at the junction of Second Polish and Fifty-Second armies, some 100 tanks of German units pushed 25km into the Polish rear, forcing its leading armoured unit to pull back and deal with this incursion. The operation fizzled out due to lack of fuel.

Red Army artillerymen prepare their 203mm B-4 howitzer to fire on Berlin. Camouflage netting was a necessary precaution, as the Luftwaffe was still capable of flying ground-attack missions. At this stage of the war no one was taking any unnecessary chances.

Hitler celebrated his 56th birthday on 20 April by decorating several Hitler Youth members for bravery and the destruction of Soviet tanks in the east. Here, boys so honoured pose for the cameras. It was to be Hitler's last public appearance. The weather that day was fine and the citizens of Berlin were issued extra rations as part of the festivities.

A shattered German anti-tank gun position, overrun by Zhukov's armour.

An unidentified ship of the Kriegsmarine fires in support of Third Panzer Army's withdrawal in the face of Rokossovsky advance. It was due to the efforts of the navy that Army Group North and the ports of Konigsberg and Danzig held out for as long as they did. Soviet naval activity in the Baltic Sea was limited.

A light anti-aircraft gun fires on Soviet troops as they advance towards Ninth Army's positions in the Spree forests. Heavily camouflaged, the vehicle is prepared to move rapidly to avoid retaliatory mortar or artillery fire.

In a hastily dug position a man of Ninth Army simply waits for the next Soviet attack. Holding lines before Berlin were of little use as the speed of the Red Army's advance hardly allowed the time to dig in. What slowed Zhukov and Konev was the wooded areas that were interspersed with waterways, which made ideal ambush positions.

The route to Berlin could hardly have been better signposted. Now with total air superiority the Red Air Force ranged far and wide shooting up any columns of vehicles heading to the west. Sights such as this were commonplace for the pursuers.

During a strangely quiet moment on the Oder sector a group of German infantrymen wait for a cup of ersatz coffee. They are all wearing the M1943 'Marsh' pattern camouflage suit.

Chapter Six

Fortress Berlin - Encirclement

On Monday, 23 April in the weakly beating heart of Nazi Germany the less-important courtiers of Hitler's regime were taking their leave. As some left, others moved in, among them were Magda Goebbels and her six children. Outside the Fuhrer bunker, across the bomb- and shell-ravaged city, Berliners waited for the battle to begin on their doorsteps.

Having fallen back on Berlin, General Helmut Weidling, commanding LVI Panzer Corps, although under sentence of death, arrived at the Fuhrer bunker to find that he was now commander of the capital's defenders. His own corps consisted of 18th and 20th Panzergrenadier divisions, the *Muncheberg* Panzer Division, the 11th SS Panzergrenadier Division *Nordland* and fragments of 9th Parachute Division. All were now at a tithe of their titular strength, therefore Weidling told off all bar 18th Panzergrenadier Division, which constituted his reserve, to strengthen the eight defence sectors. The force available to Weidling numbered approximately 45,000 army and SS men and 40,000 Volkssturm with roughly 60 tanks. It was anticipated that stragglers and more cohesive groups would swell the numbers over the next few days.

However, according to NKVD General I. A. Serov's report on the condition of the city's defences there was little for Weidling's men to stand behind: 'No serious permanent defences have been found inside the 10–15km zone around Berlin. There are fire-trenches and gun pits and the motorways are mined in certain sections. There are some trenches as one comes to the city, but less in fact than any other city taken by the Red Army.' Further comments included intelligence gained from Volkssturm POWs who told how few regular troops were in Berlin, how short of arms and equipment they were and how unwilling the Volkssturm was to fight.

Unaware of this report, troops of First Belorussian Front began to move cautiously into suburban Berlin from the north, the east and the south-east. The main thrust was an attack by Fifth Shock, Eighth Guards and First Guards Tank armies. Several units of Eighth Guards crossed the Spree and Dahme rivers in the direction of the suburb of Britz, on the Teltow canal. To their right, Fifth Shock, with the support of gunboats of the Dnieper Flotilla, also crossed the Spree.

Further west along the banks of the Teltow canal Konev's Third Guards Tank Army, supported by a colossal concentration of artillery, prepared to launch itself across this vital water barrier. Opposing them were numerous Volkssturm battalions braced with elements of 18th and 20th Panzergrenadier divisions.

The *Nordland* Division, falling back in the face of Zhukov's Guards infantry and tanks, took the opportunity to refuel its armour at Tempelhof airfield. Any possible repairs were made, and they even received armoured reinforcements. However, the bulk of the fighting rested on the weary shoulders of the infantry, and on 24 April they were launched in a series of counterattacks to push the Soviets back across the Spree river. As Weidling's counterattacks began, so did Konev's canal crossing. Soviet artillery and mortars began firing at 06.20 hrs, and 40 minutes later the first footholds had been established. Fighting desperately, the Panzergrenadiers and Volkssturm were unable to hold the line and by midday T-34s began to cross the newly erected pontoon bridges.

To the east Zhukov's troops held their ground and then counterattacked so successfully in their turn that they overran Treptow Park and reached the line of the S-Bahn railway, where they halted to regroup and bring up supplies.

Third Shock Army, approaching the outskirts of Berlin from the north-east, made steady progress passing through the infamously communist district of Wedding to reach the Schiffahrts canal.

Surrounded though Berlin was to the north-west and the west, the Soviet ring was as yet fairly porous as a group of French Waffen SS men found out as they made their way from the north, passing on the way thousands of refugees, Wehrmacht stragglers and escaping foreign workers. The French were subordinated to the *Nordland* Division just at the time it was retiring to defend Tempelhof airfield alongside the few tanks and men of the *Muncheberg* Panzer Division. This latter formation was a remarkable unit, having been formed less than two months previously around a cadre of men and machines from the Kummersdorf equipment-testing facility. Its armoured component included examples of nearly every tank and armoured fighting vehicle ever produced, including one-off experimental types. Even after the losses it had suffered at Seelow Heights and during the retreat into the city the *Muncheberg* Division could still pack a punch. But even this armoured miscellany could not hold Tempelhof indefinitely. LVI Panzer began to withdraw towards the city centre during the afternoon of 25 April. An officer of the *Muncheberg* Division described 'incessant Russian artillery fire…despite strong artillery fire the civilians population tried to escape' but more ominously the wounded soldiers were 'left where they were for fear of running into the hands of the mobile courts.' In the hell that Berlin was becoming, drumhead courts martial roamed the streets rounding up apparent deserters and hanging them from any convenient tree or lamppost with a sign describing them variously as 'traitors to the Reich', 'cowards' or any other suitable insulting epithet. The officer continued describing the cries of women and children, the whistles of Stalin Organs and the smell of death and explosives mixed with chlorine. His last words were 'The fight continues tenaciously.'

With Zhukov's forces heavily engaged around Tempelhof and the Hohenzollern–Schiffahrts canal and the Fifth Shock Army moving into the Freidrichshain district on the eastern edge of the city, First Ukrainian Front had split the defences on the Teltow canal forcing 20th Panzergrenadier Division onto Wannsee Island as its left flank pushed through the Grunwald forest towards Charlottenburg and the centre advanced driving the Volkssturm and 18th Panzergrenadier Division back towards the city centre.

Now, almost everywhere the fighting was taking place in densely built-up areas which neither the Soviets nor the Germans had experienced so seriously since Stalingrad 30 months before. Bombing and shelling had destroyed many buildings creating ready-made fortresses in which defenders could take cover and from which they could launch tip-and-run ambushes. Trams, shattered vehicles, rubble and all manner of everything to hand was pressed into the creation of barricades to block roads and junctions. Where possible, slit trenches and machine-gun or Panzerfaust pits were dug. Railway tunnels were demolished and the guns of the three immensely strong Flak towers were turned to face the approaching Soviet armour.

In the cellars of buildings German troops waited with Panzerfausts, and suddenly Soviet tank and infantry losses began to rise dramatically. Countermeasures were drawn from Chuikov's notes made during the Stalingrad campaign with updates from his recent experience of urban warfare in Poznan, and the small infantry assault group made its return.

But outside the city events were shaping somewhat differently, and in Hitler's bunker the last politicking of the 'Thousand-Year Reich' continued at fever pitch.

Part of the defences in suburban Berlin: the primitive nature of this bunker demonstrates the paucity of tools and equipment available to the garrison's construction teams. It also shows the shortage of time that Reymann and his successor, Weidling, had to do anything once the Soviets were across the Oder–Neisse rivers.

An NCO of an unidentified Waffen SS infantry formation scans the horizon for Soviet tanks on the approaches to Berlin. The ubiquitous Panzerfaust was produced and stockpiled in vast numbers. The simplicity of build and operation made it an ideal weapon for close-quarters and ambush tactics.

A quadruple-barrelled 20mm anti-aircraft gun and one of its crew under camouflage await the next sortie over Berlin by the Red Air Force. Equally useful against ground targets, this weapon could pump out up to 800 rounds per minute.

Men of Fifth Shock Army prepare to cross the Spree river on 23 April. The speed of the advance into Berlin precluded the forward movement of assault craft; therefore waterways were crossed by all means available.

A panzer IV moves through the outskirts of a village near Berlin in one of the small but vicious rearguard actions fought during the withdrawal from the Oder river line. Many such unrecorded skirmishes and localised counterattacks bought time for the city's defenders to prepare for the coming onslaught.

Gunboats of the Dnieper Flotilla had accompanied the advancing armies to provide support with the innumerable river crossings since 1944. Shallow-draught, lightly armoured vessels such as this one were ideal for close-support actions. Mounting a variety of weapons, including T-34 turrets, they could move swiftly to the aid of a tenuous bridgehead.

Young men of the Reich's Labour Service (RAD) pose valiantly for the camera before going off to join their unit. At least they already had a uniform, which was more than could be said for many of the newly formed units at this time. The Red Army was aware of the Volkssturm but regarded armed men out of uniform as bandits and therefore gave them no opportunity to surrender.

Katyusha rocket launchers of an unidentified Guards mortar unit load up for another barrage in support of Konev's forces across the Teltow canal. The effect of these weapons, nicknamed 'Stalin Organs' by the Germans, was psychological as well as tactical.

A Wespe self-propelled gun lies abandoned in suburban Berlin. Based on the chassis of a Panzer II, it carried a 105mm howitzer. On the mudguard nearest to the camera can be seen two Panzerfaust left by the crew, who appear to have taken only the machine-gun.

To increase the strength of the pickets around Fortress Berlin three NKVD Frontier Guard regiments were brought in. Here two immaculately turned-out men of 105th Frontier Guard Regiment stand watch over the entrance to a Nazi party office that dealt with Hitler Youth affairs. Both men are armed with PPSh-41 submachine-guns (smg). Their tidy appearance, including woollen gloves, indicates they have seen no action.

An extemporised distribution point in Berlin doles out fuel for those still with motor vehicles. There were several instances where supply-dump officials refused to issue food or munitions without the correct documentation, preferring to destroy their assets rather than accept no paperwork, even with the Soviets literally at the end of the street. Airfields proved useful providers of petrol and diesel.

Flying ground-attack missions over Berlin was rarely as hazardous for the pilots of the Red Air Force as it was becoming for the men on the ground. As the fighting became more confused, so the chances of death by friendly fire increased.

A German team prepares to fire its MG-42 near Berlin Zoo. The saddle-type magazine is evidence that the weapon may have been scrounged from an anti-aircraft unit, as these magazines were often used in that role. The high rate of fire, 1200 rounds per minute, made the spare barrel carried by the soldier on the left essential.

A wrecked T-34/85 is ignored by a weary section of German infantry. Judging by their clothing they are probably men of 9th Parachute Division, the remains of which were tasked with defending north-west Berlin against Zhukov's Third Shock Army. They are passing wooden anti-tank stakes.

From the attics of an apartment block Soviet submachine-gunners fire across at a German machine nest. Rooftop fighting such as this became a common feature of the street-fighting in Berlin during the last days of April 1945. The men are armed with PPSh-41 smg, a perfect weapon for this type of warfare, with its high rate of fire and ease of maintenance.

A Soviet gun crew races back to its 76mm mountain gun. Short-barrelled and man-portable, such seemingly out-of-place weapons were simple to move around the city streets and, with an elevation of 70 degrees, lethal for shooting into the higher storeys of buildings.

A King Tiger, possibly one of the vehicles of the 503rd SS Heavy Tank Battalion, sent to support SS Division *Nordland* near Tempelhof airfield. Armed with a lethal 88mm gun, it was heavily armoured, but suffered from mechanical unreliability and high fuel consumption requiring eight litres of fuel per mile. The textured material on the armour is Zimmerit paste to protect against magnetic mines.

Communications were vital to avoid confusion and death by friendly fire. Here, a pair of Soviet signallers report to the higher command on progress in the lee of a burning building. However, such was the jealousy over the victor's laurels that senior officers did not always inform their neighbours of their units' whereabouts.

Despite slight bomb and shell damage, this street in western Berlin shows no evidence that elsewhere in the city the fighting has begun. Although there is an earth barricade across the street, there seems to be a complete lack of urgency in the civilians' demeanour and that of the soldier with a walking stick. However, veterans' accounts note that some areas were almost unaffected by the war until it drove into their neighbourhood.

As the fighting intensified, the Soviets became more ruthless in their tactics. In the event of shots being fired from a building the near-automatic response was to demolish it with artillery fire. These workers' apartments have suffered little prior to the battle but now receive the attention of Chuikov's gunners.

SS Panzergrenadiers and an assault gun north of Berlin. The failure of Steiner's SS troops to mount a rescue mission led Hitler to lose faith in his elite forces. There was also a rumour among the defenders of Berlin that the SS had been secretly ordered to leave their positions and make for Schleswig Holstein. During the last days of the war, distrust between the SS and the regular army grew significantly.

All men are equal in death: Soviet and SS casualties in Treptow Park.

Elements, possibly of the *Muncheberg* Panzer Division, retire towards Berlin. The vehicles display evidence of hard fighting. The armoured side skirts on the panzers have been removed to avoid clogging of the tracks with mud or debris.

Chapter Seven

Fortress Berlin – Fantasy Armies

So far the advance into Berlin was proceeding well but German Ninth and Twelfth armies were beginning to fight back and pose problems for Konev's rear to east and west. Moscow had been lax in dealing with these formations as its focus was the battle for Berlin. However, when it came, the reaction was swift. General Busse's Ninth Army included men from XI SS Panzer Corps and V SS Mountain Corps as well as survivors of the Frankfurt garrison and V Corps, in all, upwards of 80,000 troops. The number of civilians who had attached themselves to Ninth Army was not recorded. However, Busse still had 31 tanks fuelled from abandoned vehicles. Ninth Army had been in contact with Wenck's Twelfth Army on the Elbe river. On 22 April Hitler had agreed to General Field Marshal Jodl's suggestion that Twelfth Army should be rotated eastwards from its position opposite the Americans on the Elbe and set out to rescue Berlin. Ordering General Field Marshal Keitel to 'co-ordinate the actions of Twelfth and Ninth armies', Hitler packed him off with brandy, sandwiches and chocolate for the journey to Wenck's HQ. Back in the Spree forest Busse was heavily engaged fighting off units of First Belorussian Front. Keitel reached Wenck on 23 April and delivered the order to save the capital. Hitler so lacked trust in his senior officers that he demanded that the order to save Berlin be broadcast on the national radio channel. When Keitel departed, Wenck and his staff planned their move. Part of Twelfth Army would march to Potsdam at the extreme western edge of Berlin while the greater part would head east to link up with Ninth Army. The objective was simple – to save as many soldiers and civilians as possible from the Soviet advance and then fall back to the west, where a screening force was to remain on the Elbe. When the men of the Twelfth Army were informed of this operation there appears to have been little dissent. For the people of Berlin, Wenck's arrival could not come too soon, as it was about their only hope of deliverance from the Soviets, other than the arrival of the Anglo–Americans. Indeed, so wrapped up in the fantasy was Hitler that he informed Weidling on 25 April that Ninth and Twelfth armies would 'deliver a crushing blow to the enemy'. Just what sort of blow could be delivered by two small, understrength forces that lacked fuel, armour, men and munitions was not detailed.

Wenck's XX Corps, composed of four inexperienced, newly raised infantry divisions, set off eastwards on 24 April. One of its units, the *Ulrich von Hutten* Infantry Division, headed for Potsdam, and the others for Ninth Army.

The route that both Ninth and Twelfth armies were to follow led through forests, the most dangerous points of which were the crossing of open spaces, notably the roads that ran across their path. Busse's force began its exodus on 25 April, ignoring all signals from Berlin. However, behind Ninth Army's rearguard followed Zhukov's II Guards Cavalry Corps and elements of Thirty-Third and Sixty-Ninth armies. Konev contributed Third Guards and Twenty-Eighth armies. It was a gap between these two armies that Ninth Army broke through on 26 April after bitter fighting. For the next five days Ninth Army fought its way through three lines of extemporised Soviet defence. Finally, on 1 May, Busse's advance guard linked up with Twelfth Army at the village of Beelitz. Behind them came the rest, moving, as Busse described it, 'like a caterpillar'. Roughly 25,000 soldiers had escaped, along with uncounted civilians.

Although Konev had had to switch his focus to his rear flanks the effect on the Berlin operation had not been critical.

Tactically the Soviet style had altered. Tanks no longer drove in column down the centre of a road but operated in pairs, one on each side of the road, giving cover to each other from Panzerfaust-wielding ambushers in the cellars and basements, or Molotov cocktails dropped from windows and rooftops. Supporting infantry operated in assault groups of between six and eight, armed with close-order weapons such as submachine-guns, grenades, knives and sharpened shovels. Artillery of all calibres was deployed to clear away barricades and stubborn pockets of resistance. And everywhere were flamethrowers and engineers with demolition charges for 'bunker busting'.

Late on 26 April, Tempelhof airfield was abandoned as the *Muncheberg* and *Nordland* divisions' remaining armour was ordered back to the Tiergarten. With room to manoeuvre, Chuikov projected his left flank across Konev's right, cutting First Ukrainian Front off from the Reichstag and glory. As the fighting began to close in on the central defensive area, the Citadel, German reinforcements arrived in the shape of some Kriegsmarine personnel and Latvian SS men.

Elsewhere, Spandau Prison, on the Havel river to the north-west was taken and Gatow airfield came under ground-attack. Along the Landwehr canal, Fifth Shock Army was making progress onto the Wilhelmstrasse while Third Shock Army crossed the Westhafen canal. Pushing on throughout 27 April, the Soviets reduced the German defence area to a zone 5km by 15km, which roughly ran from the Alexanderplatz in the east to Charlottenburg and the Reichssportsfeld in the west.

News, inside this enclave and outside, as Soviet control of many areas was incomplete despite their best efforts, was at a premium as the radio service had virtually ceased to function, therefore one of the major sources was the tabloid *Der Panzerbar* – The Armoured Bear, referencing Berlin's symbolic animal, the bear. *Der*

Panzerbar's headline for 26 April ran, 'The battle has reached its climax, German reserves are rushing to Berlin.' Lower down the page, a box read: 'Whoever shows cowardice over fighting like a man…is nothing but a low-down bastard.' The same day an attempt was made to relieve 20th Panzergrenadier Division but failed.

In some areas the defenders established in strongly built structures held out. On Third Shock Army's front the Stettiner Railway Station posed particular problems, as did the Schleisischer Railway Station and the Lowen Brewery for Fifth Shock Army. In these cases the Germans enjoyed the fire support of the two massive flak towers at Humboldthain and Friedrichshain respectively.

Eighth Guards Army was now responsible for flushing out German resistance in the Tiergarten, where, as various participants in the action recalled, the rhododendrons were just coming into bloom, and the Anhalter Station.

During the course of the next day, 28 April, Wenck's thrust towards Potsdam linked up with the forces stationed there and began to evacuate them to the west. Commanding a skeletal unit still called a division there was General Reymann, the officer formerly in charge of Berlin's defences.

However, the crowning moment of 28 April belonged to Third Shock Army's LXXIX Rifle Corps which, having fought its way down Alt Moabit, came in sight of the Reichstag. During First Belorussian Front's preparations for the Berlin offensive, senior officers had familiarised themselves with the landscape of Berlin by means of a massive architectural model, on which the Reichstag was objective 105.

With his empire's capital reduced to a smouldering heap, Hitler, ensconced in his bunker, continued to act as though he still controlled armies by the dozen and subjects by the million. Having decided to remain in Berlin and die, Hitler, on 27 April, having stripped Goering of all his offices for alleged treason, received General von Greim and appointed him commander of the Luftwaffe. Others, such as Albert Speer, the Minister for Arms Production, had already made their farewells. Indeed, on 23 April Speer had described Hitler as an old man resigned to death. Again on 27 April Hitler had repeated his order to Ninth and Twelfth armies that their attacks must be, 'principally to save Berlin' but no response was forthcoming. SS Obergruppenfuhrer Fegelein, brother-in-law of Eva Braun, the Fuhrer's mistress, was arrested and later executed for alleged knowledge of Himmler's plot to negotiate with the Anglo–American governments. This covert scheme of Himmler's was, for Hitler, the final straw, particularly when it was confirmed by Reuters News Agency on 28 April. Convinced there was no longer anyone he could trust, Hitler married Eva Braun and dictated his political and personal statements. Appointing Grand Admiral Doenitz Reich President, he blamed an international Jewish cabal for forcing him to go to war. Command of the army was given to General Field Marshal Schorner, who was leading the remains of Army Group Centre in Czechoslovakia. Having completed his paperwork he joined his wife, and the newlyweds retired to bed. It was Sunday 29 April.

On 25 April the American and Soviet armies linked up at Torgau on the Elbe river. This image of ordinary Soviet and American soldiers include the artist Philip Stein (famous for his Mexican mural work), who was a meteorologist with US Ninth Army and 'happene to be there'. Stein returne to the USA but the fate o the Red Army personnel open to speculation as such contact with westerners was frowned upon severely in the USS following the war's end.

Officers of Busse's Ninth Army conferring prior to the attempted breakout from the Spree Forest to link up with Twelfth Army. The success or failure of the breakout depended on the panzer troops providing the armoured spearhead; therefore much responsibility lay on the shoulders of the panzer officers such as those seen here.

As the main body of Twelfth Army made its way eastwards to link up with Busse, communications were paramount. Mobile units such as this one were essential to keep each army informed of the other's progress. Signals from Berlin urging both armies to come to the capital's rescue were ignored.

Waiting for Busse's convoy, a Soviet 45mm anti-tank gun hardly attempts to conceal itself. Light and manoeuvrable, this weapon was more than capable of dealing with soft-skinned vehicles or lightly armoured tanks at close range. The closely wooded terrain provided extra shrapnel.

An SdKfz 251/9 half-track mounting a short 75mm gun waits to take on its load of personnel before moving out from under its camouflage screen. As Ninth Army's journey progressed, such vehicles were sacrificed to provide fuel for the tanks, which were of greater fighting value.

A Soviet Maxim machine-gun team engages with a forward reconnaissance group of Wenck's Twelfth Army. Fighting was confused as the Soviets were unclear as to the objectives of both Ninth and Twelfth armies.

Shturmoviks flying ground-attack missions register on the smoke below before making their run. Three Soviet Air armies, Second, Sixteenth and Eighteenth, were committed against both Ninth and Twelfth armies. Those flying in support of Konev's forces flew over 3,000 missions.

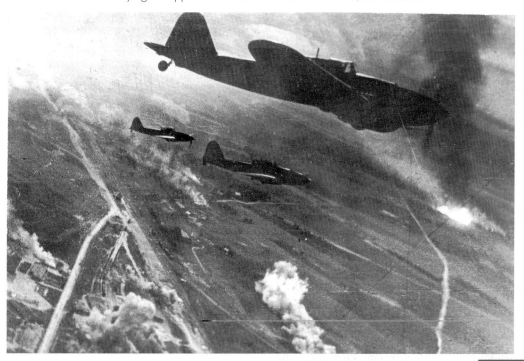

Twelfth and Ninth armies met up on 1 May. Wenck had insisted on providing as much food and transportation as he could muster for the survivors. Some were so exhausted, both physically and mentally, that they had to be beaten to their feet to receive their rations. The shuttle service to the Elbe river began that day.

Clearly showing the destruction in Berlin, this Soviet image is, to quote the original caption, of 'the tank crew of Colonel N. P. Konstantinov driving fascists out of the houses on the Leipzigerstrasse.'

This abandoned StuG IV was destroyed in the fighting with Fifth Shock Army on 27 April. The extra track pieces have been welded to the hull to give added depth to the armour.

The Soviet troops quickly developed a liking for the Panzerfaust, which they captured in large numbers. In addition to its anti-tank capabilities it was used to blast through the walls of buildings to create safe routes and to destroy bunkers. Guards Sergeant Levchenko is shown here with a Panzerfaust 100, which denoted the range in metres.

Flamethrowers were an important weapon during the street-fighting in Berlin. If available they were called into action wherever there was the least sign of resistance. This is a ROKS-2 type, designed to look like a soldier's pack so the operator was inconspicuous until the weapon was in use.

SS infantry of an unidentified unit move into the trenches during the last few days of fighting in Berlin. The man to the rear appears to be carrying a flamethrower.

The marshalling yards of the S-Bahn and national railways were difficult areas in which to fight. The open spaces were obvious killing grounds for machine-gun teams. Often overlooked from embankments or solid buildings, they were not a place for the unwary.

A Soviet assault group moves forward through the city streets. The man to the right is covering the upper storeys of a building with his PPSh-41 as the balconies could provide convenient positions for enemy infantry. As well as looking up it was sensible to look down as mines were scattered like confetti in some areas.

The calibre of the guns that First Belorussian Front brought to bear on the city's streets increased rapidly. Here a 203mm howitzer is brought into action. Capable of firing one shell every two minutes, it had a range of 16km and a crew of 15. Its tracked carriage proved advantageous in broken terrain when being towed. Apparently the target is the Air Ministr y on Wilhelmstrasse.

Gaunt, dirty and disillusioned, a group of German POWs awaits orders. Possibly some of these men would be chosen by the Red Army's Seventh Section to return through the lines and persuade others to surrender. German communist exiles and members of the so-called 'Seydlitz Army' arrived in Berlin to carry out such tasks. Clearly such a mission was hugely risky and success was mixed.

Tempelhof airfield was cleared of its obstacles sufficiently for the Red Air Force to use within 36 hours of its capture. Some 2000 German women were put to work around the clock. One of the results was the opportunity to fly out seriously wounded casualties to base hospitals in aircraft such as this converted U-2.

On 28 April, Konev, having reported his Front's progress for the day, was asked the question by Stalin, 'Who do you think is going to take Prague?' Konev replied that First Ukrainian Front was able to do this from west of Dresden. The old adage 'He who controls Prague controls Europe' may have been some consolation to the man who almost conquered Berlin.

The sight that warmed the hearts of many a Red Army veteran as it appeared through the smoke of battle – the ruins of the Reichstag.

Chapter Eight

Fortress Berlin – Collapse

The advance along Alt Moabit towards the Spree river by two infantry divisions of Third Shock Army, the 150th and 171st, had brought them, on 28 April, within 800m of the river, across which lay the Reichstag. To reach this objective they had to cross the Spree, and in front of them was the intact, inviting shape of the Moltke bridge. Barricaded and mined with artillery and machine-guns to both flanks, the bridge would not make for easy crossing, however. The task was made more difficult when, at 18.00 hrs, the Germans blew it up, but the explosives had only done a partial job and it was clearly passable on foot. Having arranged artillery covering fire, an infantry platoon, led by Sergeant Pyatnitsky, led the crossing. As the Hitlers celebrated their wedding, more and more men of both Soviet divisions crossed the river into the governmental sector, an area dotted with the monolithic ministerial buildings, many of which were heavily fortified and garrisoned. The first building that the 150th Infantry Division had to contend with was the Ministry of the Interior. As it was impossible to bring heavy guns over the Moltke bridge, hand-to-hand combat went on all morning.

At dawn on 29 April another of Fifth Shock Army's units, 301st Infantry Division, attacked the Gestapo HQ on Prinz-Albrechtstrasse. Preceded by point-blank artillery fire, two battalions overcame the defenders and planted a Red Flag on the roof. But the victory was short-lived as a fierce counterattack by men of the *Nordland* SS Division reoccupied the building.

Simultaneously, Eighth Guards and First Guards Tank armies crossed the Landwehr canal and were now within 2km of the Reichstag. The guards infantry had either swum or used improvised rafts, accomplishing the crossing under cover of a smokescreen. However, the Potsdammer bridge was captured intact by the faking of a fire on board a T-34; oily rags on its hull were set ablaze, then the crew opened fire on the defenders at close range as more tanks followed through the smoke. A dug-in Tiger I formed part of the defences as by now almost all fuel had been used up. Damaged vehicles were used as anti-tank positions until they were overwhelmed.

Chuikov's right flank was now almost opposite Weidling's HQ in the

Bendlerstrasse. Weidling, realising that the end was approaching rapidly, conferred with his senior officers informing them that Twelfth Army had reached Potsdam. Following a situation report that indicated that there were approximately 10,000 troops in the Citadel area, it was decided that a breakout towards the west would be made at 22.00 hrs the following day. Naturally Weidling had to seek Hitler's permission for the breakout and visited him the next day. Two days earlier Weidling had proposed leaving the city with Hitler under close escort but the Fuhrer had declined. Weidling's second attempt was initially refused but later in the day permission was granted as long as the escapees joined up with combat formations to continue the fight. Word of the attempt was spread as rapidly as possible. But as Weidling laid his plans, so did First Belorussian Front. Remarkably Stalin had been comparatively relaxed during the Berlin operation, allowing his Front commanders to guide matters more freely than had been the case. Possibly this light touch was the result of having surrounded the city, thereby denying access to the Anglo–American forces.

The Reichstag was the focus of attention for Zhukov and his subordinates; it was the symbolic building that he wished to present to Stalin in time for the 1 May parade in Moscow. The honour of mounting the first attack on the Reichstag fell to 150th Infantry Division, commanded by Major General V. M. Shatilov, a part of Third Shock Army. Under orders to carry submachine-guns, and having eaten a hearty breakfast prepared for them in the cellars of the Ministry of the Interior, the first wave went into the attack at 06.00 hrs on 30 April.

To reach the Reichstag the attackers had to cross the open ground of the Konigsplatz, which was cut across with a flooded anti-tank ditch some 3m wide. Heavy fire from the partially bricked-up windows of the Reichstag caused considerable casualties, which increased sharply when crossfire from the Kroll Opera House hit the attackers' right flank and rear. Cut off while other units were sent to subdue the Opera's defenders, the first assault wave hugged the ground until, a little after 11.00 hrs, they reached the anti-tank ditch. For another two hours they lay and endured fire from the Reichstag, itself under continual bombardment, until risking a further charge. Once again hit by flanking fire, this time from the flak tower in the zoo grounds, the Soviet infantry sought cover in shell holes and behind broken barricades. As they lay waiting for darkness few suspected that at 15.15 hrs Hitler and his wife had committed suicide. At 18.00 hrs Weidling was summoned to the Fuhrer bunker and told of Hitler's death. Sworn to secrecy, he was also told to forget the breakout attempt, as an armistice was about to be requested and as Berlin's commander he would be required to be present.

Less than a kilometre away from the bunker the Soviets launched their final attack on the Reichstag. Heedless of casualties and under cover of smoke, dust and the coming of darkness, three infantry regiments rushed the building with armoured support. Breaking into the vast reception hall the men of 150th Infantry Division found the defenders had either hurried upstairs or gone to the cellars. For several hours vicious fighting continued from room to room as flag bearers attempted to reach the roof.

Officially the Red Flag was planted on the Reichstag's dome at 22.50 hrs as the fighting raged below.

Six hours later General Krebs was ushered into Chuikov's HQ, where he remained while news of his appeal for an armistice was passed up the chain of command. Stalin was only prepared to offer unconditional surrender, which Krebs felt unable to accept. As May Day morning drew on and no word was received from the Germans they were given a reminder of the power they were facing as the guns of First Belorussian Front let loose a shattering bombardment. In the Reichstag and in other government buildings the battle continued into the afternoon. But elsewhere across the city isolated German units began to capitulate as the Soviet troops celebrated May Day.

At 06.00 hrs on 2 May Weidling crossed into the Soviet positions and while Martin Bormann and other of Hitler's cronies tried to make good their escape, arranged the surrender of the Berlin garrison with effect from 15.00 hrs that day.

The agreement to surrender did not end hostilities immediately. Although a recording of Weidling's voice was broadcast there were few who heard it. A leaflet-drop achieved more success and gradually the news spread across the city. However, there were those who did not wish to surrender, such as members of the foreign SS units who had no home to return to and only a cause to die for, as surrender, to them, meant, more often than not, immediate execution. Such men fought on until killed during the course of the next two or three days. Thousands attempted to escape in groups of varying sizes and with different results. Some reached Twelfth Army in Potsdam but many were rounded up by the growing cordon of NKVD and regular troops established by Zhukov to ensure that neither Hitler nor his closest followers such as Goebbels eluded capture. The hunt for Hitler and the others now proceeded apace as the population of Berlin tried to come to terms with their new situation.

A German Panzerschreck whips up the dust as it is fired. Crewed by a loader and gunner, they were the responsibility of the regimental anti-tank company, which was issued with 36. The maximum range of later models was 180m and the hollow-charge warhead could penetrate 160mm of armour plate when set at a 60-degree angle. In an urban environment such a weapon was lethal.

The smoke-filled air can almost be tasted in this image of a road junction in Berlin. The Katyusha system to the right is mounted on a US-made Studebaker lorry and is waiting for resupply, having fired off its rockets.

An SS machine-gun team fires down onto a Soviet infantry group during the last days of the Berlin fighting. The goggles are a useful addition, giving some protection against the dust and rubble that pervaded the atmosphere.

Men of Chuikov's Eighth Guards Army move cautiously through the smoke towards the Tiergarten.

A shallow communication trench running through a public park in south-western Berlin. The original caption mentions that it is a battalion HQ for a Volkssturm unit manned by regular army personnel. However, the casual demeanour of the men indicates their situation is less than dangerous.

Neatly lined up as if on parade, gunners of Eighth Guards Army pound German positions across the Spree river. The guns are 107mm M-60 howitzers firing at what appears to be maximum elevation. Although late April's weather was generally dry there were one or two rainy days.

Three Soviet ladies, smiling following liberation after years working as forced labour in Germany, peel potatoes for men of the Red Army. The problems for such men and women would come later when the NKVD rounded them up for interrogation about their activities in the Reich. For many it would mean imprisonment or death at worst, or decades of being mistrusted and ostracised at best.

The destruction wreaked on the city's infrastructure caused gas and electricity supplies to fail early on in the fighting. The restoration of such utilities was a priority for the Soviet occupation administration.

Soviet infantrymen sprint for cover near one of Berlin's many bridges. The condition of the Moltke bridge was much as the one shown here, passable on foot. Destroying bridges was often left to the last possible moment as the possibility of using them for counterattacks would thus be denied: this was regarded as defeatist and therefore a treasonable offence, punishable by summary execution.

Two of a five-gun battery of ISU-122 heavy assault guns park up for tea in a remarkably undamaged residential area in Berlin. Apparently the men are discussing where they are and where to go next. No civilians are available to question. The bicycle, near the vehicle, was a popular item of loot.

An improvised German field hospital attempts to cope with working out of doors in the lee of a gutted ruin. Medical supplies of all sorts were almost non-existent; surgery was usually performed without anaesthetic. Poison, however, was easy to obtain.

Inside the Reichstag itself the fighting continued. The forces defending this Nazi symbol included naval, SS and Hitler Youth personnel. Taken from the first-floor balcony, the image shows Soviet troops to left and right dealing with Germans holding out in the cellars.

Bringing the heavy guns of Fifth Shock Army's Breakthrough Artillery Division into the heart of the city: akin to the siege trains of earlier wars, these divisions were specialist, highly effective units. The road sign reads, 'This is the Fascist nest Berlin.' German civilians were mobilised to clear the rubble from the roads to allow clear access.

Finally the Red Flag is raised on the roof of the Reichstag by one of the banner parties. Many requests were made for the honour of raising the flag and many flags were issued; therefore it is difficult to say for certain who accomplished the feat. That it was done is sufficient.

Hitler Youth POWs shortly after their surrender. Despite the Nazi regime's attempts to involve members of the Hitler Youth in a post-war guerrilla campaign under the name of 'Werewolves', there were few incidents. However, the Soviets took the threat of such activities very seriously in the light of their own partisans' activities.

The wreckage of horse-drawn equipment that marked the passage of Busse's Ninth Army. Tanks of First Ukrainian Front were sent into the Spree Forest to hunt down the remaining fugitives. Among them may have been hundreds of former Soviet citizens of whom over 9,000 were on the ration strength of Ninth Army when it was positioned along the Oder river.

The original caption reads, 'Senior Lieutenant Nikitin reads the order of the day to his men on 1 May.' Although the fighting went on, the men were aware that the war was virtually over and many spent the day celebrating. Overindulgence in drink was not uncommon despite orders trying to contain the troops' high spirits.

The view from the Reichstag roof looking towards the Spree river and the Diplomatic Quarter: the area's main water obstacle, a flooded tunnel that acted as a moat, can be seen to the left running across the Konigsplatz. The large skeletal structure is the Lehrter railway station.

Vehicle-mounted, quadruple-barrelled anti-aircraft guns like this one gave covering fire to those troops and civilians escaping across the Havel river to Spandau. Ernest Himmler, younger brother of the infamous Heinrich, died in the stampede across the bridge.

An NCO lies close to the rear of the Brandenburg Gate while the smoke rises from the Reichstag. The badge on his sleeve indicates membership of an unidentified formation numbered 185.

Chapter Nine

Surrender

Weidling had surrendered to General Chuikov, entirely appropriately in the minds of many, as it was his valiant defence of Stalingrad that had turned the tide on the Eastern Front, but there were other armies' surrenders to consider, especially now that Berlin had capitulated, in particular, Army Group Centre in Czechoslovakia.

General Field Marshal Schorner, a particularly devoted Nazi, had signalled Doenitz on 2 May that Army Group Centre was well supplied with munitions and fuel and would head for the Elbe river. However, events overtook Schorner as Konev's First Ukrainian and Malinovsky's Fourth Ukrainian fronts bore down on his forces threatening them with encirclement. Then, on 4 May, the population of Prague rose up and broadcast appeals in English and Russian for help in ridding their country of the Germans. Schorner attempted to regain control of the city but at this point the Russians intervened. However, these were not Stalin's men but Vlasov's renegade Russian Liberation Army, which had regrouped around Prague after the debacle on the Oder. Having briefly supported the insurgents, the newly convened Czech National Council told Vlasov and his men to go. With the Soviets closing in, representatives of Army Group Centre surrendered to the Czechs in preference to Konev. Caught completely off balance, Moscow only ordered Konev and Malinovsky to move on 6 May. When Soviet overtures to Army Group Centre went unanswered a brief battle took place and on 9 May First Ukrainian and Fourth Ukrainian fronts linked up in Prague. Army Group Centre surrendered the same day, as did German units isolated at the mouth of the Vistula river.

Back in Berlin the days immediately following the garrison's surrender had been busy ones for the city's new masters. In keeping with Russian military tradition the general commanding the first troops into a city became its governor. Therefore, this honour fell to General Nikolai Berzarin, commander of Fifth Shock Army, who was appointed to the post by Zhukov on 26 April. What Zhukov and Berzarin did not know was that the city was to become an NKVD fiefdom and the NKVD owed its allegiance to Stalin and not the Red Army. Indeed, it was NKVD and SMERSH operatives from Third Shock Army, chosen to avoid any connection with Berzarin, who took responsibility for the hunt for Hitler and other high-ranking Nazis. Information regarding this matter was denied to Zhukov and his staff.

The bodies of Hitler and his wife were finally discovered on 5 May and promptly smuggled out of Berlin to a SMERSH forensic unit. Dental records confirmed the cadavers' identities two days later.

As the NKVD combed Berlin for Nazis, great and small, Berzarin busied himself with governing the city. With an army to feed and house he was remarkably tolerant towards the German population. Hospitals were opened, the utilities were restored and civilians cleared the rubble-filled streets, and corpses were buried to prevent the spread of disease as summer drew on. Indeed, when Berzarin was killed in a motoring accident the sadness of Berliners was genuine.

As well as the NKVD being beyond the control of the Red Army so too were the ministerial representatives from Moscow who arrived in Berlin tasked with the removal of as much of Germany's industrial equipment as could be taken as reparations. Entire factories were shipped to the USSR, many simply to rot by the railways in Siberia. However, alongside the nuts and bolts, intellectual property and, more importantly, the ore to produce atomic weapons were at the top of Stalin's list. Operation Borodino, the Soviet atomic research programme, was to benefit from the capture of the scientists and the plant and research undertaken at a facility south-west of Berlin, but the Soviet scientists' particular need was uranium. The home of Germany's atomic research was the Kaiser Wilhelm Institute, which was captured on 25 April. Although much had already been evacuated before the NKVD cordoned the area off, '250kgs of metallic uranium, three tons of uranium oxide and 20 litres of heavy water' were discovered there, which amounts were adequate for the Soviets' immediate requirements. Other sources of uranium lay in Saxony and Czechoslovakia, now also accessible to the USSR, but only after the peace treaties had been signed.

During 2 May on Germany's Western Front the provisional German government under Grand Admiral Doenitz published directives that continued the war against the Soviets with the simple intention of allowing as many Germans as possible to escape to the west. War with the Western Allies would continue only where they disturbed this policy. The same day the remains of Army Group Vistula surrendered. The next day Ninth and Twelfth German armies east of the Elbe river opened negotiations with American Ninth Army and began to cross to the west in significant number on 4 May. Simultaneously, Field Marshal Montgomery accepted the surrender of all German forces in Holland, Denmark and northern Germany. General Field Marshal Jodl, as Doenitz's representative, was sent to meet with Eisenhower at his HQ in Rheims. Unable to avoid unconditional surrender, Doenitz ordered Jodl to sign a total capitulation document with effect from midnight on 8

May. At midday on 7 May Doenitz ordered all commanders on the Eastern Front to 'fight their way through the Russians if they had to' but above all to head for the west as soon as possible. Furthermore, all hostilities against the Western Allies were to cease. Jodl also obtained a statement from Eisenhower's Chief of Staff that the Wehrmacht High Command would not be held accountable should 'individual soldiers and some units' disobey the surrender order.

Signatures were affixed at 02.41, one of which was that of General I. Susloparov, the Soviet representative attached to Eisenhower.

Livid, Stalin insisted on a ceremony in Berlin as the Red Army was still fighting Army Group North in Courland and Army Group Centre in Czechoslovakia.

On 8 May Britain's Air Chief Marshal Sir Arthur Tedder, with Lieutenant General Carl Spaatz from the USA and General de Lattre de Tassigny, representing France, arrived in Berlin at the same time as Jodl and the German delegation. At Zhukov's HQ the Allies signed the act of surrender, followed by the Germans, who then left the city. The deed was done and the celebrations began; the battle for Berlin and Europe ended at 23.01 hrs on 8 May 1945.

A lone Soviet soldier stands and considers the view. As the original Soviet caption says, 'So here it is, the f*****g Reichstag.'

A T-34/85, festooned with sprung metal frames to repel or detonate Panzerfaust rounds, and displaying its Allied air recognition markings, joins a traffic jam at the Brandenburg Gate. The post-battle silence led to many men having difficulty sleeping until they adjusted to the new conditions.

The business of mine and munitions clearance went on for weeks after the fighting had ended. Soviet engineers are seen here cautiously working their way up a street using the tips of their bayonets to check the ground. Soviet troops were very wary of German booby-traps, and their propaganda units had been at pains to warn the men about casually selecting souvenirs to send home in their monthly 5kg parcels.

Der Fuhrer, Adolph Hitler, pictured here in happier times, was by April 1945 a shadow of his former self. Portrayed in his 'Political Uniform', he proudly displays his Iron Cross 1st Class awarded in August 1918 when serving in the German Army. Unlike Stalin, Hitler had bitter experience of front-line service.

Soviet officers inspect what is described as 'Hitler's globe'. The area of interest is Africa. Sightseeing generated anger in the minds of many Soviet troops as they found it hard to understand how such comfortably off, well-fed people as the Germans obviously were should want to invade the USSR, where the standard of living was considerably lower.

The streets of Berlin presented a grim contrast with the city's pre-war splendour.

This wounded, elderly German, possibly clutching goods bought at the black market that flourished near the Brandenburg Gate (to his rear), watches with resignation as a column of Soviet tanks rolls down the Unter den Linden. The lead vehicle is an IS-1 with a 122mm gun.

The Military Governor of Berlin, General Berzarin, in the centre of the group, was liked and respected by Berliners. He was described by one commentator as, 'fat, with sly, brown eyes and prematurely white hair. He is very clever, very balanced and crafty.' He was obviously an ideal candidate for the position. Rumour laid his 'accidental' death at the door of the NKVD.

As peace spread, so did the rewards for men of the Soviet Armed Forces. Here members of the Dnieper River Flotilla are presented with medals by a senior naval officer.

Soviet officials view a fallen Nazi eagle while treading on a photograph of Hitler.

One of the more gruesome relics of Hitler's rule was this execution block discovered in the Gestapo offices when Poznan fell to Chuikov.

A common sight across Europe in the spring of 1945: a group of displaced persons trekking somewhere under the flimsy protection of a white flag.

Reprisals were not limited to Germany. This public summary execution was carried out in Belgrade.

Alleged German war criminals, when located, were often returned to the town or city where they had carried out their crimes. One such group is being hanged in front of a large crowd. Justice was being seen to be done.

In their hundreds of thousands German POWs marched east. Some would not return to their homes for a decade. As well as coping with POWs the Soviet government was faced with the task of repatriating an estimated 4,000,000 former Red Army troops and civilians deported to the Reich as slave labourers. Stalin's son Yakov, captured in 1941, was not among them.

Zhukov signs the German surrender document in Berlin on 8 May 1945. The bespectacled man is Andrei Vyshinsky, the USSR's Deputy Foreign Minister, better known as the prosecutor at the Moscow show trials of the late 1930s that so damaged the Red Army immediately prior to the outbreak of war.

Red Army men sit comfortably on part of one of the monuments near the Brandenburg Gate. For some of them it was the end of an odyssey that had started on the banks of the Volga river in Stalingrad.

German women queue for work as nightclub hostesses in a newly reopened bar. Possibly the poster gives some indication of their duties.

Sitting in the May sunshine a group of German POWs awaits shipment east.

Montgomery, Eisenhower, Zhukov and de Lattre de Tassigny in Berlin for the victory parade.

This shattered T34/76, probably built between 1941 and 1942, has fallen victim to some of Berlin's anti-tank defences.

On one of Berlin's waterways or lakes a group of German combat engineers prepares for a hit-and-run mission against Soviet forces. The weapon held by the central figure is an M44 assault rifle.

With mixed facial expressions denoting their emotions members of a section of the National Labour Service's female branch (RADwJ) prepare to mount their bicycles and support their male defenders by delivering messages or other tasks. Wartime conditions resulted in members of the RADwJ remaining with this organisation longer than in earlier years.